US AFRICA COMMAND, CHANGING SECURITY DYNAMICS, AND PERCEPTIONS OF US AFRICA POLICY

By Stephen F. Burgess[*]
2008

OVERVIEW

This report will demonstrate that U.S. change agents in seeking transformation focused inwardly within the bureaucracy. They did not bother to consult with African leaders and made assumptions about African reactions to AFRICOM which demonstrated a lack of empathy. The authoritarian leadership style of Secretary of Defense Donald Rumsfeld brought about an —order that could not be refused," including the unfortunate directive that AFRICOM headquarters should be placed on the African continent. The directive was rejected by most African leaders and media.

A subsequent —strategic communications" campaign to repackage AFRICOM and sell it to African leaders failed because of already established suspicions. Only the reversal of the directive to place the command on the continent brought grudging acceptance, along with US offers of training exercises and other forms of security assistance. Change agents within a bureaucracy must be careful to consult with foreign actors in attempting to bring about transformation.

While African reaction to AFRICOM was largely negative, there was variation in types of responses. Some leaders in sub-regions and states feared terrorist attacks against an AFRICOM base that would undermine their regimes. Others feared the possibility of regime change. Sub-regional powers objected to US military presence in their areas of hegemonic control. Ideology was important, with non-aligned states rejecting AFRICOM and more liberal and pro-Western states accepting it. A second conclusion is that African states are weak. Those states that do not align themselves with the United States feel threatened by it.

The negative lessons of 2007 demonstrate that Africa Command and US diplomats should continue engaging with regional players in order to explain the purpose of the new command and react to feedback. Thanks to considerable US diplomacy in 2008, African perceptions of US security policy and strategy in Africa and of US Africa Command have shifted from largely negative to mostly positive.

INTRODUCTION

In 2006, US Secretary of Defense Donald Rumsfeld launched the process of creating a US Africa Command (AFRICOM) to take over the areas of responsibility in Africa from US European Command (EUCOM), US Central Command (CENTCOM), and US Pacific Command (PACOM).[1] Towards the end of 2006, as he was leaving office, Secretary Rumsfeld charged an implementation planning team with putting the process in motion; directed that AFRICOM reach full operational capability on October 1, 2008; and ordered that a headquarters be established by

---

[*] The opinions expressed in this paper are those of the author and do not necessarily reflect the opinions and policies of the U.S. Air War College, the U.S. Air Force, the Department of Defense, or any other branch of the US Government. The paper is approved for public release; distribution is unlimited.

that date –on the African continent".[2] In February 2007, President George W. Bush and the new Secretary of Defense Robert Gates approved Rumsfeld's initiative, including the directive to place AFRICOM headquarters on the continent. An interim command began building the organization and scouting possible locations on the continent for a headquarters. US officials began the process of informing African leaders about AFRICOM and attempting to persuade them that the new command was in Africa's best interests and that it posed no threat to Africa. However, US officials encountered unexpectedly stiff African resistance to AFRICOM.

Throughout 2007, African resistance to AFRICOM grew, partly due to the looming prospect that a US combatant command of hundreds of military personnel would be placed on the continent. This prospect came in the wake of the 2003 US invasion of Iraq and the 2006-7 US-backed Ethiopian invasion of Somalia. In addition, many African leaders were upset that they had not been consulted before the February 2007 announcement. Subsequently, in each of the sub-regions (west, east, north, southern, and central), many leaders and media commentators spoke out against AFRICOM.[3] Resistance culminated in a January 2008 African Union (AU) summit in Addis Ababa, Ethiopia, when AFRICOM was a matter of discussion. However, member states refrained from passing a resolution condemning the new command, which meant that the process of creating AFRICOM could realistically continue without African censure.[4]

In the wake of the AU summit, US officials pressed on towards AFRICOM's full operational capability on October 1, 2008. However, in response to strong African resistance to the prospect of an enhanced US military presence on the continent, the directive to place an AFRICOM headquarters somewhere in Africa was shelved.[5] Even more modest proposals for AFRICOM –regional integration teams" or –regional offices", which would work with sub-regional organizations, were dropped.[6] It was hoped that these changes would make it easier for AFRICOM to engage with African countries and regional organizations.

With the end of plans to expeditiously place AFRICOM headquarters on the continent, resistance diminished in some African countries, and with offers of training and other forms of assistance, states began to engage AFRICOM. Even so, AFRICOM faces an uphill struggle to succeed as a combatant command. It is probable that Congress will not be wholly convinced about AFRICOM's strategic importance and will not provide adequate funding; and African leaders will be disappointed at the command's inability to provide the level of training and other services that EUCOM and CENTCOM do presently for African countries.

Two fundamental questions for this report are: why did US officials behave the way they did in authorizing and announcing the establishment of AFRICOM? And why did many African leaders strongly resist the creation of AFRICOM?

This report examines strategic challenges in the standup of AFRICOM and changing US-Africa security relations. In addressing the research questions, foreign policy decision-making and implementation cases as well as theories, models and hypotheses are examined and utilized in helping to explain the way in which AFRICOM was formed as well as negative African reactions and helping to predict the future of AFRICOM and US-Africa relations and more specifically how AFRICOM might relate to regional actors in Africa and assesses how it might shape efforts in East, West and Southern Africa. This report draws on interviews with US and African officials and experts. The focus of interviews has been on Southern, East and West Africa; these are the three sub-regions with —anchor states" (i.e., South Africa, Nigeria, Kenya and Ethiopia);[7] relatively effective sub-regional organizations [the Southern African Development Community (SADC), Economic Community of West African States (ECOWAS), and the East African Community (EAC)] and influential newspapers and other media. These sub-regions play a strong role in shaping leadership views and opinions that inform the African Union. A special focus has been placed on South Africa, which is the most powerful and influential African state, where the strongest resistance to AFRICOM occurred and has persisted and on neighboring Botswana, which has accepted AFRICOM.

CONSULTATION AND NON-CONSULTATION IN FOREIGN POLICY IN DECISION-MAKING

Cases from the literature on foreign and security policy decision-making and implementation provide theoretical concepts, models and hypotheses in explaining AFRICOM's unilateral establishment and non-consultation of African leaders as well as generally adverse African reactions.

In terms of consultation with external actors before policy decisions have been made, there are significant cases, including consultation by the United States as the only superpower with external actors. For example, US officials consulted NATO allies in order to gain legitimacy before bombing Serbia in 1995 and 1999 in Operations Deliberate Force and Allied Force. US officials consulted UN Security Council members in order to gain authorization for the use of force before attacking Iraq in January 1991 and in March 2003. These and other cases demonstrate the importance of securing legitimation in US foreign and security policy decisions.

As will be explored in this report, it appears that US officials did not feel that legitimation was important in regard to AFRICOM and assumed that African leaders trusted the United States. This assumption was based upon more than a decade of engagement by EUCOM and CENTCOM in Africa. It also indicates a lack of empathy on the part of decision-makers.

From another perspective, Africa has been of relatively low importance to the United States. Therefore, the possibility of negative feedback and even rejection by African leaders did not appear to decision-makers to present significant costs to the United States.

The most prominent case of foreign policy decision-making, which involved non-consultation with other actors, was the Cuban missile crisis. The Kennedy administration worked in secrecy for more than a week to arrive at a decision before it began engaging with the Soviets. From his examination of the decision-making process, Graham Allison generated the —governmental (bureaucratic) politics" model to explain why the decision-making process led to the compromise —embargo" decision that was made and not to the more —rational" or realist decision of attacking Cuba and Soviet forces that was initially favored by the Joint Chiefs of Staff and others.[8] JFK managed to avoid choosing air strikes against Cuba, which were being urged on him by his military advisors, by seeking to generate alternative courses of actions through convening a team of foreign policy and national security experts in the Executive Committee (EXCOM) of the NSC. The Cuban missile crisis demonstrates that, when the stakes are high and the costs of a bad decision can lead to disaster, leaders often seek other ways of deliberating to reach an alternative decision and course of action. The crisis was bilateral with no great need for multilateral legitimation of the US decision. Obviously, in the AFRICOM case, the stakes were far lower, though decision-makers also felt no need for legitimation and proceeded without consulting African leaders and regional organizations.

After President Kennedy announced the US course of action, he made certain that the Soviet Union was informed in regard to US decisions and the implementation process, because the costs of non-communication could have been nuclear war. In this sense, the US decision-making process conformed to the realist —rational actor model" in which state actors behave in accordance to their interests.[9] Similarly, once the decision was announced and resistance mounted, US officials also felt the need to reach out to African states and organizations in order to avoid rejection and thereby sustain the AFRICOM project.

In 1971, the Nixon administration did not consult with its allies when it ended the gold standard for the US dollar. After internal deliberations, the administration arrived at a unilateral decision, which the administration announced and implemented. Afterwards, the administration conciliated with angry European partner nations whose currencies had suddenly been devalued. However, there was no threatened massive retaliation from Europe, and President Nixon timed the announcement to bring political advantage to his administration.[10] In contrast, the AFRICOM case involved lower stakes and apparently did not involve political advantage for the Bush administration. Even though the stakes were lower and there was no political advantage to be gained, African states were still not consulted.

Inside the decision-making bureaucracy, the salience of bureaucratic actors can make a difference in the decisions that are made. Those with high salience will demand access to the decision-making process. A case in point is the Law of the Sea Treaty in the late 1970s. Inside the decision-making bureaucracy, the US Navy pressed for a 12-mile limit of sovereignty in opposition to proposed 200-mile zones. During this period, the US government supported the Law of the Sea Treaty. Once the Navy had secured US government agreement, then the Navy's salience lowered, and less powerful actors, such as deep sea mining companies, emerged to lobby against and effectively block US acceptance of the treaty.[11] This switch in salience levels occurred before the United States finally rejected the Law of the Sea in 1983. When the United States did so, some governments were angered, having expected to be consulted about US intentions.

Within the AFRICOM decision-making bureaucracy, the salience of the Office of the Secretary of Defense and especially the OSD-Policy branch appeared to be significantly higher than that of other actors within DOD and the State Department.[12] It would appear that OSD-Policy timed its push for AFRICOM as Rumsfeld was deciding to leave office and wanted to finish incomplete projects and perhaps leave a legacy.[13]

In the 1990s, the issue of NATO expansion was debated within the Clinton administration and was the subject of considerable bureaucratic infighting, led by National Security Adviser Anthony Lake and Assistant Secretary of State for East European Affairs, Strobe Talbott. Lake was able to use his proximity to President Clinton to help win the argument for NATO expansion.[14] Once the decision to expand was adopted, the Clinton administration was able to convince member states of NATO to agree and Russia to accede. The member states generally did not find their interests threatened by NATO expansion, so there was little or no resistance. Russia was in a weakened state and could only protest.

There was bureaucratic maneuvering by OSD-Policy to gain the acceptance of Secretary of Defense Rumsfeld and other senior leaders that AFRICOM was a fundamental part of transformation. However, AFRICOM proponents did not anticipate the level of resistance that would arise from African leaders, who were intended beneficiaries of the AFRICOM initiative.

US Africa policymaking has traditionally been centered in the bureaucracies of the State and Defense departments due to the relative lack of importance of Africa to interest groups and Congress.[15] Therefore, the OSD was able to proceed with the formation of AFRICOM without fear of domestic opposition. The State Department could have voiced its opposition but was not headed by strong advocates for the department's previous lead role in Africa. Secretary of State Condoleezza Rice and Assistant Secretary of State for Africa, Jendayi Frazer, agreed with the AFRICOM initiative and cooperated with DOD. As for Congress, it was in the habit of granting most DOD funding proposals in the wake of September 11, 2001 and agreed to initial DOD requests for AFRICOM.

Another factor to consider is the leadership style and psychology of the chief foreign and security policy actors and ability to set the agenda.[16] The chief agenda-setter and decision-maker in this case, Secretary Rumsfeld, operated in an authoritarian and unilateral manner.[17] Rumsfeld's drive for the ―transformation" of DOD, the military, and the way in which the military was deployed throughout the world colored many of DOD's actions during his tenure.[18] According to Robert D. Kaplan:

> Parts of the world were unassigned when Rumsfeld came into office; he assigned them. He created Northern Command for the defense of the continental United States and put Canada and Mexico inside it. He assigned Russia to European Command and Antarctica to Pacific Command. Out of part of European Command, which was responsible for much of Africa, he created Africa Command—a potentially path breaking bureaucratic instrument that incorporates other agencies like the State Department and emphasizes bilateral training programs and indirect, humanitarian-affairs-oriented approaches over combat. As obvious as all these choices seem, they weren't when Rumsfeld made them.[19]

Leadership style and agenda-setting models combined with the governmental (bureaucratic) politics model provide a plausible explanation of the decision-making process.[20] Rumsfeld was able to ―frame and set the agenda", and Ryan Henry of OSD-Policy and Theresa Whelan of OSD-Africa worked hard with high salience within the bureaucracy, were supported by an authoritarian Rumsfeld, and were able to do so with minimal questioning and objections from other agencies and the president.

The governmental (bureaucratic) politics model posits that actors must overcome bureaucratic resistance through decisive political action. The problem is that decisive action often comes without multilateral consultation, which leads to the inability or difficulty to implement the decision internationally. In terms of salience and expected utility, a bureaucratic political victory appears to have been treasured more by OSD than a foreign policy success in winning over African leaders. When the stakes are low, it appears that actors tend to engage in governmental (bureaucratic) politics first and then explain their decisions to foreign actors later. It seems that there is a need to gain acceptance within the bureaucracy for a foreign policy innovation, such as AFRICOM, and to look for bureaucratic victories.

In the AFRICOM case, the most applicable hypotheses are: (1) actors within a foreign and security policy bureaucracy seeking change on a low priority matter are less likely to consult non-adversarial outside actors than those seeking change on a high priority one, which may involve the use of force. (2) In order to accomplish an organizational goal, actors within an agency often may have to act within the foreign and security policy bureaucracy before consulting with international actors. (3) An agency head's leadership style is more likely to determine whether consultation will take place or not. (4) Actors are more likely to push an initiative when decision-makers are seeking change than preserving the status quo. (5) Unilateral decisions are less likely to produce positive results in the international arena than multilaterally derived ones.

FOREIGN AND SECURITY POLICY DECISION-MAKING AND REACTION TO POLICY CHANGE

A realist explanation for African leaders' resistance to AFRICOM focuses on threats to state (and regime) survival.[21] Any move to increase presence by the great powers, especially the American superpower, is perceived by those leaders as an existential threat. Realism, which holds that the survival of states (and regimes) is fundamental, helps to explain why states resist foreign policy change that might be threatening. Coming four years after US Central Command had carried out the invasion of Iraq and overthrown Saddam Hussein; many African leaders appeared to be concerned about their fate with the possible insertion of the new command on the continent. The US-backed Ethiopian invasion of Somalia in December 2006 further amplified those concerns.

The United States went through a similarly painful learning exercise in 1996 when it announced that it would lead in the creation of an African Crisis Response Force that would respond to Rwandan-style genocide and Somali-type civil war. African states rejected the paternalistic US proposal, and the Clinton administration had to go back to the drawing board.[22] Similarly, it seemed that AFRICOM represented the creation of a large new combatant command that would be inserted into one country in the African continent. The presence of more than a thousand US service personnel and the ability to call in thousands more would immediately pose a threat to the surrounding countries.

Some states, such as Liberia, Botswana, Mali, and Rwanda, were favorably disposed towards AFRICOM.[23] The variation in reaction across states, where some accept and others reject can be explained by the degree of commitment to the ideology of —nonalignment" with the —West". The more committed a regime is to non-alignment; the less likely it is to support the expansion of a US presence on the continent. Non-alignment arose among those leaders who did not want to be part of the US-led anti-communist camp.[24] Those states that did not embrace non-alignment included those that were already aligned with France (e.g., Mali) or with the United States (e.g. Liberia). Botswana was led by pragmatists who did not sever links with Britain and who forged close links with the United States as part of the development process and in order to prevent absorption by South Africa in the 1960s.

A related hypothesis is that anchor states are more likely to oppose outside threats to their dominance than smaller states that are receptive to cooperation with outside powers.[25] Another related hypothesis is the degree of pride of various leaders (indicated by the length of time a leader has been in office) determines acceptance or non-acceptance of external interventions, such as the placing of AFRICOM on the continent. The longer a particular leader is in office and the more powerful the state, the greater the estimation of his importance and the more he expects to be consulted on decisions such as AFRICOM. For example, in Zimbabwe, President Robert Mugabe has been in power for twenty-eight years, has long been a leader within SADC and the African Union and has rejected AFRICOM, partly because it is an affront to his self-conception as an African leader. In contrast, Liberian President Ellen Johnson-Sirleaf is a new leader with less pride and is more accepting of AFRICOM.[26]

US COMBATANT COMMANDS AND AFRICOM

Besides the literature on foreign policy decision-making and implementation, the cases of formation of US geographical combatant commands provide insights into AFRICOM's formation and the negative responses of many African leaders. US combatant commands have been created in the aftermath of wars or US military engagement in regions. In creating and sustaining US geographical combatant commands, US interests and threats to those interests have been crucial in decisions made by DOD and Congress. With the Goldwater-Nichols DOD Reorganization Act of 1986, greater authority and resources were given to the geographical combatant commands.[27] In 1990-1, CENTCOM demonstrated the new potential of combatant commands in Operation Desert Shield/Desert Storm.

PACOM and EUCOM were created in the aftermath of the Second World War. PACOM was created in 1947 to sustain US military efforts in the Pacific after the Second World War and was based on the World War II command in the Pacific. PACOM dealt with growing Soviet involvement in the Pacific. After the victory of the Chinese Communists on the mainland, PACOM became involved in the defense of Taiwan against the Peoples Republic of China. After North Korea invaded South Korea, PACOM played a role in the defense of the South. PACOM became responsible for mutual defense treaties with the Philippines, Japan, Australia, New Zealand and Taiwan. PACOM also became engaged in Southeast Asia and the Vietnam War. After the end of the Cold War, PACOM became engaged in struggles over Korea and Taiwan. It remains a most important command that is fully funded by Congress. The reaction to PACOM in Asia and the Pacific was not negative among non-adversarial Asian states due to US presence during the Second World War and its aftermath.

EUCOM was created in 1952 on the basis of US World War II organization in Europe and provided logistics, maintenance and administrative support to the Supreme Allied Commander Europe (SACEUR) and the Supreme Headquarters Allied Powers Europe (SHAPE). EUCOM's task was to help sustain US military efforts in post-World War II Europe, especially in defense against the Soviet Union and in the transition of West Germany to a democratic state with a revived military that could assist in the defense of Western Europe. EUCOM was especially important in engaging with NATO. After the end of the Cold War, EUCOM has remained important in NATO expansion and military operations in the former Yugoslavia and Afghanistan. It was a most important command that was and is fully funded by Congress. The reaction to EUCOM in Western Europe was minimal due to US presence during the Second World War and its aftermath. In the 1980s, much of sub-Saharan Africa was included in EUCOM's area of responsibility in the Unified Command Plan (UCP). At the time, there was little or no resistance by African leaders against EUCOM activities in Africa. There were few comments about the —neo-colonial" connotations of a —European" command operating in Africa.

CENTCOM was founded in 1983 in the wake of President Jimmy Carter's Rapid Deployment Joint Task Force (RDJTF) in March 1980 and his pledge to maintain a US presence in the Gulf to deal with threats to the flow of oil, including revolutionary Iran and the Soviet Union, and to counteract the Soviet invasion of Afghanistan and other possible threats to the oil flow. CENTCOM remained a relative backwater until the Iraqi invasion of Kuwait in 1990. Since then, CENTCOM has become the most —combatant" of the commands and has been fully funded by Congress. Since September 11, 2001, CENTCOM has been in charge of fighting wars in Afghanistan and Iraq (as well as dealing with Iran, oil, Saudi Arabia, Egypt, and Al Qaeda). The reaction to CENTCOM in the Gulf and Middle East was minimal due to US presence in the 1970s and 1980s. CENTCOM only became an issue in the Gulf and Middle East in 1990 with the Gulf War and by then it was well-established. The Horn of Africa was added to CENTCOM's area of responsibility, and there was little or no African resistance to CENTCOM entry into the region. There were few protests to CENTCOM and the establishment of the Combined Joint Task Force-Horn of Africa after September 11, 2001 and its operations in Djibouti, Kenya, and Ethiopia.

PACOM, EUCOM and CENTCOM have been well-funded by Congress due to their strategic importance in dealing with threats to US national security interests. However,

SOUTHCOM was never as strategically important and has not been fully resourced. SOUTHCOM was founded in 1963 in the wake of the Cuban missile crisis and Soviet entry into the region in order to manage US military engagement in Central and South America. Well before 1963, Latin American states were accustomed to US military presence in Panama and Cuba and intervention in Central America and the Caribbean, so the creation of SOUTHCOM did not generate much protest. Many leaders were quite familiar with US presence in the region. In contrast, a new generation of radical leaders was violently opposed. In terms of funding, there were never any substantial or existential threats to US national security interests in the SOUTHCOM area of responsibility, so it was never funded adequately by Congress, and SOUTHCOM continues to struggle today.[28]

Given the preceding analysis of geographical combatant commands, it would appear that AFRICOM was created at the wrong time and was proposed to be located in the wrong place. DOD assumed the legitimacy of combatant commands without doing the proper homework for AFRICOM, which demonstrates a lack of empathy.

DOD CREATES AFRICOM: DECISION-MAKING AND PRONOUNCEMENT

In the 1990s, officials in the Office of the Secretary of Defense broached the AFRICOM idea as DOD engagement in Africa and peacekeeping training and exercises increased.[29] The seam between EUCOM and CENTCOM in Africa grew problematic for DOD.[30] A low-level debate began over whether an Africa Command should be created as a fully fledged combatant command or as a —sub-unified" command under EUCOM.[31] The opportunity to push the creation of AFRICOM came with the Bush Administration and Secretary of Defense Rumsfeld. Transformation became the guiding principle in 2001 and was reflected in the Quadrennial Defense Review (QDR).[32] Part of the QDR included the shifting of US forces and a willingness to redraw the Unified Command Plan including the founding of AFRICOM. DOD expressed the intention to move troops and operations out of Germany a decade after the Cold War and into Eastern Europe or home to the United States. The Department of Defense was determined to downsize EUCOM. Russia was shifted into EUCOM's AOR. The new emphasis on Eastern Europe and Russia meant that less attention could be given to Africa. In addition, in 2002 and 2003, Secretary Rumsfeld's reference to Germany as part of the —old Europe" set in motion the idea to move EUCOM's Africa operations out of Germany and more onto the African continent.[33] According to Robert D. Kaplan:

> …by 2004, the Pentagon unveiled plans to bring home an additional 70,000
> troops from those fixed garrisons, even as it moved to expand a network of bare-
> bones sites in Asia, Africa, the Middle East, and Latin America to support
> rotational rather than permanently stationed forces. Such —lily pad" bases would

10

be different from the ―Little Americas" of the Cold War: no soldiers' spouses, no kids, no day-care centers, no dogs, no churches. A leaner presence might prove less of an impediment to bilateral relations. The number of status-of-forces agreements with host countries doubled from the end of the Cold War through the end of Rumsfeld's tenure, from 45 to over 90. And the Air Force signed more than 20 comparable gas-and-go agreements with countries in Africa while Rumsfeld was secretary of defense.[34]

The 2005 QDR continued emphasizing the transformation of US deployments, especially with the ongoing ―war on terror".[35] Also, the genocide in Darfur and US airlifting of African peacekeepers shone a spotlight on the seam between CENTCOM (Sudan was in its area of responsibility) and EUCOM (Chad, Nigeria, Rwanda and other states were in EUCOM's AOR). From 2004 onwards, EUCOM and US Air Forces Europe (USAFE) found itself airlifting AU peacekeepers and their supplies in CENTCOM's AOR. The seam provided ammunition for OSD officials, such as Principal Deputy Assistant Secretary of Defense for Policy, Ryan Henry, and Deputy Assistant Secretary of Defense for Africa, Theresa Whelan, to push for the creation of AFRICOM.

In August 2006, as Secretary of Defense Rumsfeld was preparing to leave office, he gave orders for the creation of AFRICOM. ―The command must be fully operational by October 2008 on the African continent". The new command would have ―inter-agency structure and content". The US government failed to consult African leaders as AFRICOM was being conceived and created in the latter half of 2006. With Rumsfeld's resignation at the end of 2006, President Bush and the new Secretary of Defense Robert Gates sustained support for the creation of AFRICOM, and Congress provided the seed money. US officials began the process of searching for locations for AFRICOM headquarters and AFRICOM regional offices on the continent.

In early February 2007, the Bush administration announced the creation of AFRICOM with an emphasis on US interests, especially in fighting the war on terror. Soon after the announcement, US officials, including several general officers, sought to justify AFRICOM's existence. The emphasis on US interests and the lack of consultation with African leaders and media immediately led to an intense backlash against AFRICOM. Rear Admiral Robert Moeller, the executive director of AFRICOM's transition team, told the press that the motivation behind creating AFRICOM was the increasing importance of Africa strategically, diplomatically and economically…to the United States.[36] In a briefing, Principal Deputy Assistant Secretary Henry told the media that the command ―will focus on some efforts…to defeat or preclude the development of terrorists or terrorists' networks."[37] Deputy Assistant Secretary Whelan told the press that ―Afca is of significant strategic importance to the United States….its natural resources…you can see our main objectives include defeating terrorists."[38] As late as the end of April, Ryan Henry stated the US formula for establishing AFRICOM included fighting terrorists in Africa, countering Chinese diplomacy on the continent, and gaining access to Africa's natural resources, especially oil.[39]

DOD officials initially stated that AFRICOM would be a *combatant* command, one that would command US forces in combat. Lieutenant General Walter Sharp, Director of the Joint Staff, advised that while ―many of the missions of AFRICOM will be non-kinetic…AFRICOM will also be responsible for any necessary military action in Africa.‖[40]

African Reaction to AFRICOM

In February 2007, the announcement of AFRICOM gave rise to widespread protests from African leaders and the media, while some leaders either welcomed the new command or reserved judgment. A widely expressed comment was, ―China is bringing factories, infrastructure to Africa, while the US brings the military.‖ In South Africa, pro-western newspapers responded to the announcement with the following comments: ―AFRICOM's advent follows a pattern of extraordinary military expansion under George Bush; it makes China's business oriented policy look like a corner shop.‖[41] Another comment stated that ―the creation of AFRICOM is a belated admission that the world changed in 1989 not in 2001; it's the US that's playing catch-up to global and continental realities.‖ [42] Another comment was that ―the possible creation of AFRICOM contains a notable omission: the word ‗oil.‘‖[43]

Thus, many African leaders and media outlets believed that the US action in establishing AFRICOM had little to do with altruistic reasons and more to do with selfish motives of establishing access to oil and natural resources; enabling the United States to fight terrorism; and countering China's growing influence on the African continent.[44]

Some saw the United States unilaterally establishing and announcing the formation of AFRICOM without prior consultation and input from African states as a sign of arrogance and condescension.[45] Others believed that AFRICOM represented another attempt by a bellicose United States to achieve military domination and that US intervention in Iraq and Afghanistan (and Somalia) could be repeated in Africa. Leaders and the media were concerned that AFRICOM's presence on the continent would increase conflict and terrorism on the continent.[46] Another viewpoint was that AFRICOM was unneeded and that a multilateral approach with the regional economic communities, the African Union and the United Nations was the only viable approach to help Africans solve problems and that the unilateral approach by the United States, represented by AFRICOM, was unneeded and unwarranted.[47]

The rejection of AFRICOM did not stem from widespread anti-Americanism but rather from the reluctance of leaders, the media and public opinion has stemmed from fears concerning

US hegemony in Africa.[48] The Pew Global Attitudes Survey has indicated that the US image in Africa remains generally positive.[49]

In West Africa and ECOWAS

The response to AFRICOM was mixed with some negative and some positive reactions. In Nigeria, the government and media were generally negative. An editorialist wrote, ―It is gainsaying to mention that Africans will be seeing US marines and soldiers more often than not," and referred to President Bush as ―an emerging Hitler whose primary motive is to extend his influence." [50] A second commentator called into question the security assistance role of the new command ―ARICOM does not proffer answers to the growing tide of conflicts that inflict the beleaguered continent; rather it raises a lot of queries."[51] A Nigerian commentator writing in a South African newspaper noted that the US failure to provide meaningful assistance to Liberia during its violent civil war belied any notion of a genuine altruistic intent.[52] He continued that AFRICOM was evidence of US neo-colonialist ambitions.[53]

In 2007, Nigeria refused to host AFRICOM for a number of reasons including a fear that the United States would infringe upon Nigeria's sovereignty over oil.[54] In contrast, Liberian President Ellen Sirleaf-Johnson took a positive position toward AFRICOM and stated that its role would be ―conflict prevention, rather than intervention." [55] The Liberian president was the only African leader to openly extend an invitation to establish AFRICOM headquarters on African soil. In response, the newly elected Nigerian President Umaru Yar'adua warned Liberia not to accept AFRICOM, and Nigeria as the regional hegemon influenced ECOWAS not to accept the new command.

In Southern Africa and SADC,

The response was mostly negative.[56] South Africa, Zimbabwe, Angola, and Namibia were especially opposed due to their ―national liberation" heritage and commitment to non-alignment. These SADC states believed that any US involvement in Africa should be from a distance and not on the continent.

South Africa's opposition to AFRICOM derived from its position as the regional power in SADC and primary leader within the African Union.[57] South Africa's unwillingness to host AFRICOM in Southern Africa has little to do with popular dislike of the United States.[58] Jakkie Cilliers of the Institute for Security Studies in Pretoria stated that South Africa might be leading the SADC move against Africom, ―not so much because we don't like the US, but because we want to be the big boys".[59]

South Africa's foreign policy is based on the African National Congress' historical experience, including the US policy of constructive engagement with the apartheid regime in the

1980s, which still resonates today. The ANC remains committed to the Non-Aligned Movement and relations with anti-western states. The US invasion of Iraq offended the South African government and brought widespread criticism, including from Nelson Mandela. At the same time, the South African government has been willing to work with the United States in some areas but not in others.

In July 2007, South African Defense Minister Mosiuoa —Terror" Lekota warned against AFRICOM on the continent, even though he admitted that —ARICOM was not really a new development". South Africa proceeded to lobby the African Union to take a position opposed to AFRICOM and its location on the continent. US Ambassador to South Africa, Eric Bost, complained that Lekota was not responding to embassy requests to meet General William —Kip" Ward, the recently nominated commander of AFRICOM.[60] In a presentation at a South African university, Ambassador Bost and Theresa Whelan bluntly told a high level South African audience that AFRICOM was going to be created and that there was little that South Africa could do to stop it. The controversy heightened South African opposition to AFRICOM.[61]

In February 2007, Botswana expressed interest in engaging AFRICOM, though it was reluctant to make a commitment of host AFRICOM headquarters. At the time, an independent newspaper in Botswana criticized AFRICOM but did not reject it: —Btswana has yet to work out position on AFRICOM, since it was not consulted by US on command structure."[62] However, the article went on to say, —ARICOM does not bode well for the continent, says editorial; US military installations on African territory would mortgage away sovereignty; Botswana should stay clear."[63]

Since South Africa and other SADC states stated their opposition to US forces in Botswana, the government was reluctant to host AFRICOM because to do so would create dissension within SADC.[64] South Africa put pressure on Botswana and other SADC states not to host AFRICOM.[65]

In East Africa

Views about AFRICOM were mostly negative. In Kenya, the media commented that AFRICOM is exactly the opposite of what we need; it will tilt countries toward military responses to issues that need patience and diplomatic approaches. —How different Chinese and US approaches to assuring oil flow are!" Bush has embarked on a righteous goal with altogether counterproductive methods.[66]

Another criticism of the Kenyan media was based around the US-backed Ethiopian invasion of Somalia and the activities of CJTF-HOA in the region. One editorial stated that the

—USs using Somalia and neighboring countries to conduct experimental tests on the effectiveness of its new military outfit, AFRICOM."[67]

Based upon political considerations and criticisms of AFRICOM from the media and civil society, the Kenyan government did not accept US requests to host AFRICOM. In contrast, Ethiopia as a US ally was favorable towards AFRICOM but could make no commitments to host the command due to the location of African Union headquarters in Addis Ababa. The one state in East Africa that warmed to AFRICOM was Rwanda, which enjoyed a robust security cooperation relationship with the United States and which even entertained the idea of hosting AFRICOM headquarters.[68]

In Central Africa

The attitude was mixed. Gabon explored the possibility of hosting an AFRICOM regional office. Gabon's patron, France, took an ambivalent position towards AFRICOM, ultimately opposing any physical presence in its sphere of influence. The most militarily powerful actor in the neighborhood, Angola, was opposed to an AFRICOM presence because of the regime's historical experience in opposition to the United States and its current ambivalent attitude towards the superpower.

In North Africa

Leaders and the media were negative mainly due to the prospect of AFRICOM posing a terrorist target for Al Qaeda.[69] This was especially true for pro-Western Morocco and Tunisia. In Morocco, the Justice and Development Party warned against making the country a —battle ground" between US and its —enemies" if the government decided to host AFRICOM.[70]

In Algeria, the attitude towards AFRICOM reflected a fear of terrorism and a commitment to non-alignment. In March 2007, US Under-Secretary of State for public diplomacy, Karen Hughes, visited Algeria and discussed AFRICOM with the government. Afterwards, Algerian Minister of Foreign Affairs Mohammed Bedjaoui denied that Algeria received a request from the US to establish military bases on its territory as a part of plans for an Africa Command in 2008 and said —Algeria will not accept American bases on its territory."[71] Algerians noted the US unwillingness to offer anti-terror cooperation to Algeria when it was plagued by terrorist violence in the 1990s.

In non-aligned Libya, officials rejected idea of any foreign power establishing military bases anywhere in Africa after meeting with US officials.[72] Libya and to a lesser extent, Algeria, refused to host AFRICOM because of a desire to maintain sovereignty over its internal affairs and to keep the United States out of African affairs.[73] Widespread was concern was expressed in regard to sovereignty over oil and gas operations.[74]

15

RESPONSE TO REJECTION: US "STRATEGIC COMMUNICATIONS" CAMPAIGN

By May 2007, the United States and DOD responded to negative attitudes towards AFRICOM with a "strategic communications" campaign to win over African leaders and media. US officials, especially in OSD-Policy, crafted a less-interest based message about AFRICOM, which emphasized the interagency and non-kinetic side of AFRICOM. In particular Ryan Henry found it necessary to meet with prospective hosts to eliminate misconceptions about AFRICOM.[75]

The revised AFRICOM message was meant to assuage the fears of African leaders, as US officials began to travel the continent. US officials stressed that AFRICOM "partnerships" would assist organizations and states to meet security challenges and provide training and coordination in counterterrorism, peacekeeping, and disaster relief. However, as a result of the campaign, the Bush administration began to send out conflicting messages regarding AFRICOM that reached African officials and created confusion. A significant obstacle to establishing and selling AFRICOM was the failure of the Bush administration to clearly and sufficiently articulate AFRICOM's mission. Unfortunately, AFRICOM's mission remained vague to Americans and Africans alike.[76] Some of the confusion about AFRICOM's mission was due to the fact that there were too many Bush administration officials speaking about AFRICOM's mission and their messages were consistent.

In a briefing by an OSD-Policy official in May 2007, it was asserted that AFRICOM would be interagency and non-kinetic.[77] In July 2007, Secretary Theresa Whelan declared that "Afican command is not going to reflect U.S. intent to engage kinetically in Africa…this is not about fighting wars."[78] Whelan failed to define the terms "non-kinetically" and "kinetically," a failure that may likewise have caused problems in communicating a clear message to Africans.

On August 1, 2007, Assistant Secretary of State Jendayi Frazer testified that unlike other unified commands, AFRICOM would integrate personnel from DOD; the Department of State; and US Treasury, Commerce, and Agriculture and that AFRICOM's unique structure would be an opportunity to capitalize on the strength of these organizations, enhance unity of effort, and integrate and synchronize operations under one command authority.[79]

In September 2007, Theresa Whelan informed the press that "instead of saying war fighting is the primary mission of the command…we are saying the primary mission of this command is to focus on building security capacities in Africa"[80] and "the primary objective is not to fight and win wars on the continent."[81] By using the terms "primary mission" and "primary objectives", Whelan implied that war-fighting was a mission and objective, albeit not a primary mission or objective, of AFRICOM. Additionally, by using the phrase, "we are saying," she was

16

conveying the fact that the United States was being less than candid about AFRICOM's primary mission.

On September 21, 2007, Theresa Whelan asserted that it was untrue that AFRICOM was an attempt to further expand the war on terror in Africa, secure oil reserves, or hedge against Chinese influence in Africa.[82] President Bush echoed Whelan's assertion noting that AFRICOM was established to ―help Africans achieve their own security, not to extend the scope of the war on terrorism or secure African resources.‖[83] However, such statements about the basis for the United States' standup of AFRICOM were contradicted by previous statements that the following were part of the US calculus for establishing AFRICOM - US access to Africa's national resources and oil; the US desire to thwart terrorism; and China's growing influence in Africa.

On September 28, 2007, General William Ward, then the AFRICOM commander-designee, told U.S. senators at his confirmation hearing that ―it [AFRICOM] will focus on tasks that include…counter-terrorism efforts.‖[84] Thus, messages about AFRICOM remained contradictory.

In October 2007, AFRICOM achieved initial operational capability, as a sub-unified command under EUCOM at Kelly Barracks, Stuttgart, Germany under the command of General Ward. The deputy commanders were Ambassador Mary Carlin Yates and Rear Admiral Moeller. AFRICOM was short-staffed and was executing while planning. Congress remained supportive, but long-term funding for AFRICOM remained questionable. AFRICOM began working towards becoming fully operational in October 2008. By mid-2008, it was clear that the directive that AFRICOM would have inter-agency structure and content had not been fulfilled. Although AFRICOM was primarily ―non-kinetic‖ in its mission, it was granted the status of a ―combatant‖ command with the potential to use force.

TOWARDS AFRICAN ACCEPTANCE OF AFRICOM

By the start of 2008, most African leaders still did not know what AFRICOM was and why it should be on the continent. At the January 2008 African Union meeting in Addis Ababa, member states discussed AFRICOM but did not pass a resolution against the command. On February 21, 2008, President Bush commented that that it was simply not true that ―all of a sudden America is bringing all kinds of military to Africa.‖[85] While his statement was technically true, AFRICOM does not represent a U.S. effort to bring ―all kinds of military to Africa,‖ AFRICOM does represent a U.S. militarization of Africa—a militarization that causes anxiety among Africans.[86]

US adjustments and diplomacy began to produce results and states began to work with AFRICOM.[87] The May 2008 announcement that AFRICOM would not be placed on the African continent led to even more states accepting the new command. Significantly, once the United States decided not to base AFRICOM on the continent, Nigeria changed its stance and accepted AFRICOM. This was indicated by Nigeria's hosting of Operation African Endeavor in July 2008 - an interoperable communications exercise.

SOUTH AFRICAN ATTITUDES TOWARDS AFRICOM AND US SOUTH AFRICAN RELATIONS[88]
Government Attitudes

Attitudes of the South African government and those of individual officials remain negative towards US Africa Command (AFRICOM). These negative attitudes persist even after AFRICOM announced that the command headquarters was not being placed on the African continent, which had been the most contentious issue that had set many African states against AFRICOM. A prominent sign of this negativity was South Africa's rejection of participation in ―Afrca Endeavor‖, a multinational exercise focusing on interoperable communications and information systems sponsored by AFRICOM in Nigeria.[89] Also, South Africa boycotted a peacekeeping and law enforcement training center in Botswana, because it involved AFRICOM funding.[90] Just as telling, though seemingly trivial, was the South African Department of Defense rejection of correspondence regarding US International Military Education and Training (IMET) funding for South African National Defense Force (SANDF) personnel, because it appeared on AFRICOM letterhead.[91]

An indication in the field research of South Africa's negative attitude was a SANDF brigadier general's question at a symposium regarding whether or not the United States was still trying to ―smuggle‖ AFRICOM onto the continent.[92] This question came after it had been made clear in the symposium (and three months after US officials had announced) that AFRICOM would no longer seek to place a headquarters or regional offices on the continent.[93] The question followed a query by the same brigadier general on Nigeria's hosting of Africa Endeavor, an indication that AFRICOM was gaining increasing acceptance in African countries and that the South African government had come to the realization that opposition to AFRICOM on the continent was fading.[94]

At the same symposium, a South African Department of Foreign Affairs United States desk officer criticized the United States and AFRICOM for wanting to come to South Africa in order to conduct counterterrorism training. Instead, South Africa and other countries wanted a broad range of security and peacekeeping training. He concluded that the United States was not shaping AFRICOM to meet the needs of African states.[95]

Criticisms were leveled against the way in which AFRICOM was presented in South Africa by US officials. In particular, at the same forum in July 2007, Deputy Assistant Secretary of Defense for Africa Theresa Whelan attempted to explain that AFRICOM was not going to be a traditional —combatant" command like CENTCOM or EUCOM. Instead AFRICOM would be largely —nonkinetic" and would engage in development activities. When the audience expressed skepticism about AFRICOM and Whelan's assertions, a US official retorted that AFRICOM was being established with or without the consent of African states. A year later, some South African officials and remember the —take it or leave it" attitude of some US officials and remain uncertain about what AFRICOM will do.

In regard to improving relations, the Department of Foreign Affairs official said there was a need for both the United States and South Africa to listen to each other and identify common interests. At present, it was difficult for diplomats to communicate US intentions to South Africa and South African intentions to the United States. There was hope for improving the communication process and the working relationship between the United States and South Africa, especially with the prospect of cooperating in the reconstruction of Zimbabwe.[96]

In response to a comment that South Africa's negative reaction to AFRICOM was being driven by the —ideology of non-alignment",[97] the Department of Foreign Affairs official defended South African adherence to non-alignment and South-South relations. South Africa still wants to be able to determine its own foreign policy objectives, including non-alignment. Unfortunately, the United States sees non-alignment as a threat and overreacts, with a —you are against us" syndrome. Instead of reacting so negatively to South Africa's foreign policy, the United States needed to respect the non-aligned perspective in the development of AFRICOM.

OPPOSITION TO AFRICOM FROM THINK TANK EXPERTS AND ACADEMICS

South Africa has by far the greatest concentration of think tank experts on the African continent; it also has a large number of university researchers who focus on African security issues.[98] Think tanks and their experts are important in that they advise the South African government and other governments as well as SADC and the African Union on policy matters. Some also advise the donor community (e.g., the European Union and European governments) and international nongovernmental organizations (NGOs). Therefore, they are an important voice in South African and international civil society. A majority of think tank experts and university researchers interviewed opposed AFRICOM and offered rational arguments for why it was a bad idea.[99]

One argument expressed was that AFRICOM represented an escalation of the war on terror in Africa, which was not in Africa's interests. Another argument was that new wave of military intervention on the African continent. The US invasion of Iraq in March 2003 and the US-backed Ethiopian invasion of Somalia in December 2006 were widely mentioned as portents

19

of US intervention using AFRICOM. The invasions created fears that the United States would mount interventions to overthrow regimes, such as the Mugabe regime in Zimbabwe, which the United States did not like. Also, counterterrorism and torture were mentioned as reasons to oppose AFRICOM. The fear has been that AFRICOM would help to bring further US counterterrorism activities to more parts of Africa.[100]

Another criticism of AFRICOM was of the "3D" concept. The concept of cooperation among diplomacy (State Department), development (US Agency for International Development) and defense in order to dry up support for extremists and terrorists has been adopted by the US government and particularly by the Combined Joint Task Force-Horn of Africa (CJTF-HOA) in cooperation with USAID and the US Embassy in Nairobi.[101] The criticism from think tank experts and others is that the military dominates because of the preponderance of resources and the large "D" of the military swamping the much smaller "Ds" of diplomacy and development. The critics believe that AFRICOM will dominate the diplomatic and development instruments of power in Africa.[102] Several experts recommended that the United States should move away from the militarization of foreign policy and engagement.[103]

AFRICOM is also burdened by its moniker – a "combatant command". The question from think tank experts and university researchers is - what is AFRICOM going to "combat"? In dealing with this sort of question, the United States should make it clear that AFRICOM is merely to be used to enhance peacekeeping capabilities and skills in the context of technical cooperation and building capacity.

The United States and Africa need to engage in dialogue to establish common interests before AFRICOM will be well-received. The United Nations also needs to be supportive of AFRICOM for it to succeed.[104] The United States needs to rethink its modes of engagement. The African Union and sub-regional organizations would have been more responsive if the United States would properly engage.[105] The United States and AFRICOM need to work properly with regional security organizations, such as SADC and ECOWAS, if AFRICOM is to be successful. It is also important to engage with civil society throughout Africa. Unfortunately, Assistant Secretary of State for African Affairs, Jendayi Frazer, had only one video teleconference with civil society while AFRICOM was being sold to South Africa.

In regard to individual think-tank experts, Adekeye Adebajo, a Nigerian and Director of the Centre for Conflict Resolution, criticized the United States and AFRICOM on a number of fronts.[106] He believed that AFRICOM will become a reality, but there is a deeper issue at stake. There are suspicions about the US war on terror, with 2,000 US troops in Djibouti;[107] violation of rights by US backed anti-terrorism policy, which is being used to clamp down on internal dissent in African states. US gunboats have launched missile attacks against Somali civilians, which make AFRICOM and US military policy in the Horn of Africa problematic. There is a need for —regime change" in the United States and a new start for AFRICOM. The same problem was evident in the case of the African Crisis Response Force in 1997, which the United States attempted to impose on Africa. The deeper problem is that the United States and AFRICOM are not trusted. There is a need to deal with deeper issues of trust. Some governments may temporarily work with the United States, but African civil society will remain skeptical and reluctant to engage. Governments are not necessarily taking public opinion into account when they cooperate with the United States. Adebajo believed that the United States has overestimated the threat of terrorism in Africa. Currently, there are lots of questions that remain to be answered in the war on terrorism. Terrorists may be using Somalia, Sudan and other territories in Africa, but the way that the war on terror is being handled is counterproductive. In conclusion, the United States needs global support in the war on terror.

Richard Cornwell of the Institute of Security Studies (ISS) in Pretoria - Africa's leading security think tank - commented that AFRICOM was not well sold and that the US campaign to sell AFRICOM came in the wake of EUCOM Deputy Commander General Charles Wald and his —all-white staff" who were not very diplomatic in their approach to African states. General William —Kip" Ward replaced Wald and was more diplomatic but has much fence-mending to do.

SUPPORT FOR AFRICOM

Support for AFRICOM in South Africa came from think tank experts and university researchers that are generally pro-West, such as Greg Mills of the Brenthurst Foundation (supported by the Anglo-American Corporation).[108] The argument of Mills and others is that South African leaders think ideologically and not strategically, which disadvantages the country in the pursuit of its interests, especially economic interests throughout Africa. A new generation of South African leaders needs to be taught to think strategically. They need to move beyond ideology and find realistic ways in which South Africa can advance in the world and Africa be made more secure.[109]

Mills commented that AFRICOM was clearly an example of bad US public relations. However, South Africa will have to eventually swallow its pride and accept AFRICOM for a number of reasons, especially the deterioration of the South African National Defense Force (SANDF). Currently, South African officials think that AFRICOM is about —imperialism" and are suspicious of US motivations. There are divisions within SADC that have opened wide over AFRICOM, Zimbabwe and other issues. For example, Tanzania, Zambia, and Botswana tend to accept AFRICOM and want to see dramatic change in Zimbabwe.

Francois Vrey and Abel Esterhuyse, professors at the South African Military Academy, believe that AFRICOM is badly needed in an Africa which is not secure and not capable of securing itself.[110] They see a lack of capacity by African militaries and African regional organizations to keep the peace in Africa and the need for significant external assistance including AFRICOM. It is important to note that African regional structures are largely beholden to foreign funding, including from the United States.

For example, piracy is a major problem that African states and organizations are not capable of dealing with, while AFRICOM has the capacity to do so. Africa can provide troops and hardware for peacekeeping on land but not on the sea. African militaries tend to be very land-centric. Vrey and Esterhuyse commented that African governments have impressive rhetoric about working together to bring peace and stability in weak African states and to combat piracy and other security problems. However, the actual implementation at the operational level is poor. African states need partnerships with entities such as AFRICOM to work to bring about peace and stability and to build capacity through training and other measures.

Therefore, to reject AFRICOM with a broad brush is not wise due to the fact that most states do not have the capability to operate. Most Africans do not care where the assistance comes from, but African politicians make it an issue. Vrey and Esterhuyse surmised that Africa is characterized by the —ubuntu" concept where all leaders are friends with each other and reluctant to take responsibility for Africa's problems. In regard to South Africa's rejection of AFRICOM, they attributed it to South Africa's position as the leading power in Africa and the regional hegemon in Southern Africa. In addition, South African leaders objected to the United States —backed the wrong horse" during the Cold War and opposed the African National Congress. The role of ideology plays an important role and is manifested in anti-Americanism, including among military students.

According to Vrey and Esterhuyse, the Chinese are more involved in Africa militarily than the United States and AFRICOM, and China is providing arms to Zimbabwe. US interests are greatest in the Gulf of Guinea with some of the largest projected oil reserves in the world, and those interests may conflict with Chinese interests. The United States needs to go beyond the polemics of African leaders to the next level where reality dictates that things have to function. The United States and AFRICOM also need to work with multinational oil and mining firms in the provision of security. Of particular interest is AFRICOM working with Nigeria and Shell in stabilizing the Niger Delta and off-shore oil operations.

The bottom line is that many African leaders do not understand that AFRICOM is just a command structure that cannot operate outside the bounds of US foreign policy. They do not know what AFRICOM is, what it can and cannot do. Many leaders are hampered by anti-Americanism.

VIEWS FROM NEUTRAL INTERVIEWEES

A number of neutral interviewees still had reservations about AFRICOM. Gavin Cawthra,[111] Director of The Centre for Defence and Security Management, University of the Witwatersrand, manages courses that focus on education and training in security management, and the Centre supports institutions all over the SADC region. He commented that the negative response to AFRICOM makes it difficult for engagement and exercises, education and training, especially at the SADC level. Many still view AFRICOM as primarily about counterterrorism training rather than broader security training.[112] AFRICOM has been tainted by poor conceptualization and consultation. It makes it difficult to build cooperation. The problem is that SADC, led by Angola, Zimbabwe, Namibia and South Africa, has the most ideological perspective compared to all of the other regions. Similarly, Naison Ngoma,[113] an ISS researcher, is heading a security sector reform project and sees AFRICOM as a potential source of assistance in the security sector reform process in many African countries.

AFRICOM and private military companies was a subject of interest for Francois Vrey and Abel Esterhuyse. For the US Africa Contingency Operations Training and Assistance (ACOTA) peacekeeping training program and for peace support operations, private companies have been essential. They could cover the entire continent, providing training and security.[114] However, the United States and AFRICOM may be more cautious with contractors after the mixed experience with Blackwater in Iraq.[115] They observed that the private security sector in Africa is led primarily by ―Westerners" (i.e., whites) who work and get things done, much like AFRICOM. Nevertheless, they concluded that the United States and AFRICOM should seriously consider working with private military companies.

US FOREIGN POLICY AND US-SOUTH AFRICAN RELATIONS

US foreign policy in Africa invoked a number of different views, as did US relations with South Africa. Critics of US foreign policy in Africa were especially concerned about US policy in the Horn of Africa.[116] Richard Cornwell of ISS commented that a problem was getting the Department of State and the Department of Defense to talk and act together, especially in Somalia. The United States greatly overestimated the ―terrorist threat" in Somalia. In his estimation, the country with its menagerie of warlords could never produce a Taliban that could harbor Al Qaeda and attack the United States. Cornwell asserts that Assist Secretary of State Jendayi Fraser engaged in a dangerous policy in supporting the Ethiopian invasion and the overthrow of the Islamic Courts Union. The invasion has created a monster, which could give radicals a global orientation to attack the United States. He commented that CJTF-HOA ―hearts and minds" campaign and the drilling of boreholes have been nullified by US Somalia policy. The United States should have allowed the Islamic Courts Union to stay in power and continue to unify the country. Cornwell was also critical of US policy towards Sudan, which has led to the contractor Pacific Architects and Engineering (PA&E) getting kicked out of the country. Now there is no one to do base construction for UNAMID/AMIS. US leaders did not think through the consequences.[117] In addition, one critic commented that US Africa policy was all about ―curing sick Africans" and ―fighting terrorism" and not about attending to the majority of Africans.[118]

Supporters of US foreign policy in Africa see the need for greater US involvement, including AFRICOM, due to the convergence of a number of factors, including the need for greater security and development. In addition to AFRICOM's role in enhancing African security, Greg Mills said that US trade with Africa is the long-term strategic instrument to bring greater development and security and to improve US-African relations. Aid has not been as promising; even Millennium Challenge Account aid, which insists on good governance, is not necessarily a good instrument. The shift towards trade and away from aid in Africa is exemplified by two trends - the shift to liberal political doctrine and electoral democracy as well as the shift to liberal economic orthodoxy. A prominent anti-apartheid activist in the 1980s, Renfrew Christie, saw China and Iran teaming up with certain African states against the United States; therefore, AFRICOM would be an important addition to African and American security interests in dealing with Iran, China and other adversaries.[119]

SOUTH AFRICAN FOREIGN POLICY AND RELATIONS WITH THE USA

Viewed from the opposite angle, comments were varied about South Africa's foreign policy and its relations with the United States. Positive comments about South African foreign policy were made by a number of think tank experts, who also criticized the United States and AFRICOM. Garth le Pere and Chris Landsberg[120] (as well as DFA personnel) were supportive of South Africa's ambitious foreign policy under President Thabo Mbeki. They defended South Africa's commitment to non-alignment as well as the country's lead role in founding the African Union (AU) and the New Partnership for African Development (NEPAD). South Africa's initiatives had raised the profile of the country on the world stage and placed the country at the head of other African states. In their minds, the assertive foreign policy of Thabo Mbeki promoted South Africa's national interests.

Negative comments about South African foreign policy were made by Greg Mills who said that it is plagued by a lack of strategic vision. The AU and NEPAD and African Renaissance were not in the broader strategic interest of South Africa. In order to grow the economy and integrate into trade networks and maximize the national interest. In an op-ed in the *International Herald Tribune,* Mills made the following comments:

> Mbeki never demonstrated that he possessed a clear understanding of South Africa's national interest or how to balance ideological considerations and the country's priorities in trade, investment and international politics.
> At the United Nations, for example, short-term tactical politicization routinely overshadowed strategic considerations. Instead of leading the African voting bloc, the UN's biggest, on trade access and help to the continent, South Africa blocked UN managerial reform, obstructed the interests of Western powers and maneuvered around tougher action on Burma, Zimbabwe and Iran. None of this did one bit for Africa or Africans.
> The anti-imperialistic tenor of Mbeki's foreign policy was understandable, given his background. Less explicable was his failure to apply to Russia and China the same opprobrium he reserved for the West, especially the United States. Whatever the issue, under Mbeki South African opposition to U.S. policies often appeared more reflexive than considered.[121]

Mills also said that no one in the South African government or other governments has focused on critiquing the destruction of the Zimbabwe economy through terrible policy choices. The critiques have only been in the political realm, regarding Robert Mugabe's abuses of power.

Vrey and Esterhuyse said that the real threat to South African interests is increasing Chinese involvement in construction and mining industries throughout Africa. However, South African politicians have not reacted to this trend, which threatens the country's economic well-being.

Richard Cornwell of ISS said the reason why South African leaders opposed the United States and AFRICOM was because of —no-Stalinist Cold War" thinking.[122] South Africa and Africa are overestimating their influence. Africa accounts for only 1.5% of global trade and has a GDP equivalent to Belgium's. Therefore, South Africa (and Africa) needs to work more closely with the United States and the West. Nonalignment is an illusion; the United States could merely turn its back on South Africa and Africa and return to a pre-9/11 policy of neglect. The United States has been working to create a —League of Democrats", of which South Africa could be a part. However, South Africa prefers non-alignment and has voted against condemnation of Burma in the UN Security Council, voting with Russia and China, and worked to prevent Omar al-Bashir, Sudan's dictator and architect of the Darfur genocide, from being handed over to the International Criminal Court.

PROSPECTS FOR CHANGE: THE UNITED STATES

In general, there was speculation about the November 2008 elections and how it would affect US relations with South Africa. There was disagreement over Barack Obama, with some claiming that, if elected, he would bring sweeping change in US-South African and US-African relations and with others claiming that only cosmetic changes will be made. Several interviewees were skeptical about change. Gilbert Khadiagala, head of the department of international relations at the University of the Witwatersrand, commented that what will bring change is a broad-based educational campaign in South Africa and the rest of Africa to explain the role of Congress and other institutions in the making of US foreign policy.

American experts in South Africa see a change in US administration as presenting an opportunity for improved US-South African relations. Brooks Spector, [123] a former US Information Service officer, argued for dramatic improvements in US public diplomacy. Spector was filled with ―mystified horror‖ watching the AFRICOM saga unfold. Eighteen months later, the United States realized the need for more intensive public diplomacy. US official did not understand the cultural dynamic with the innate suspicion of what the United States wants to do. Many South Africans think that the United States has a base deep in the heart of Africa and a strike force poised for action anywhere on the continent; that the United States invaded Iraq for oil; and that the United States has a naval base in Equatorial Guinea to protect its oil interests. With all these known facts, the United States did not have a logistics issue but a public relations issue. There was no sounding of public opinion, with officials assuming that AFRICOM was a bureaucratic exercise of rearranging the map; instead, AFRICOM was a public relations nightmare. The ―3D‖ approach to peacebuilding is seen as even more surreptitious, fed by the ―transformational diplomacy‖ initiative by the Department of State, which supposedly ―militarizes‖ development policy and programs.

Spector recommends crafting a public relations strategy for AFRICOM and US-South African relations. A major part of that strategy would be engaging with South African media, especially print media, which is sold over half of Africa and whose internet news sites have global dissemination. South Africa has good professional media people who can sell the story if properly informed. It would be crucial to have media appearances by locals as well as Americans. The new administration, if it decides to keep AFRICOM, needs to spread good will throughout Africa as quickly as possible, and then spend several years to promote the command. The United States needs a skilful diplomat as ambassador to South Africa to repair relations. Public diplomacy must deal with meta-themes and engage with intellectuals and not focus solely on HIV/AIDS.

Francis Kornegay, [124] a US Africa expert working at the Centre for Policy Studies, also argued for improved US public diplomacy, especially regarding AFRICOM. He also called for the United States and AFRICOM to assist in the building of African unity through the African Union, sub-regional organizations, and the African Standby Force. The United States and

AFRICOM should start over by engaging with the AU Peace and Security Council and with South Africa and Nigeria and other continental leaders to establish dialogue in an open-ended discussion of the notion of partnership. Kornegay also recommended shifting foreign policy decision-making power back towards the State Department and development policy back towards USAID, which would make AFRICOM a supporting command.

In regard to the prospects for change in South African foreign policy now that Thabo Mbeki is no longer president, there were a variety of views.[125] The end result is that Thabo Mbeki will no longer be leading foreign policy.[126] He has been replaced by a less outward-looking leader and government, which is likely to be more pragmatic. While prospects for improved US-South African relations do not look good, there are those who believe that a Zuma administration will lead to improved relations and perhaps even to the acceptance of AFRICOM. Brooks Spector predicts that a Zuma administration will be pragmatic like the Mandela one and that the ideologues of the Mbeki government will be replaced. There are those who believe that the foreign policies of both countries will be more pragmatic and amenable to improved relations and that it will end the ―liberation movement club" (Zimbabwe, Namibia, Angola, Mozambique, South Africa). Greg Mills commented that ―if the new administration in Pretoria can unshackle itself from the ANC's inhibitive liberation ethos, Mbeki's departure from office could revitalize South Africa's standing in world affairs."[127] Another factor to consider is the decline of educated elites at the pinnacle of power will mean that South Africa could be less capable in managing foreign affairs. South Africa will become less assertive in its foreign policy.[128]

Zimbabwe appears on the road to change, with agreement on power-sharing, though it is difficult to predict what will happen. The reconstruction of Zimbabwe holds out the prospect for significant and substantive US-SADC cooperation. The United States can help in the reconstruction of Zimbabwe. A number of experts recommended that the United States should engage with SADC and that AFRICOM should exercise with SADC military forces including those of Zimbabwe. The current policy of boycotting SADC by the United States is counterproductive. There are those who believe that if the transition of power is completed in Zimbabwe and if the United States and EU lift sanctions, it will become easier for the United States and European Union to deal with SADC. They may have a role to play in reviving the Zimbabwean Defense Force.

Other experts believe that the counterterrorism focus of AFRICOM will make it difficult to work with SADC and other actors. It was better when the US focus was on ACRI and ACOTA peacekeeping training and not so much on counterterrorism training.[129] Education and training for security among policymakers and practitioners in SADC region. CDSM preparing a ten year impact study. Funding for security education might come from USAID.

The United States could help in the building of security strategies in South Africa and SADC. South Africa lacks a security strategy, and there is a need to develop strategic thinking. The SADC Organ on Defense, Politics and Security is plagued by the lack of transparency and a clear strategy is needed. Furthermore, it is difficult to know how decisions are made within SADC.

In regard to the issue of whether the United States and AFRICOM should engage primarily with states or with regional organizations, viewpoints varied. Greg Mills said that the US government needs to differentiate its policies, because each state has its own needs and challenges. The next generation will start to look like Asia, with good performers (Singapore and Rwanda) as against bad performers. The United States should engage with good performers before sub-regional organizations. In regard to AFRICOM and working constructively with African constituencies. The US style of international conduct is anathema to the South African government. The United States should build internal constituencies like the African Center for Strategic Studies (ACSS) alumni sections – an approach which has succeeded for ACSS. The United States needs to work more with political players; thus far, there has been too much focus on engaging with the military.

WHY THE SOUTH AFRICAN NATIONAL DEFENSE FORCE (SANDF) NEEDS AFRICOM

The deterioration of the South African Air Force, Navy, and Army has reached crisis proportions. Helmoed Roemer Heitman of *Jane's Defense Weekly* commented on the deterioration of the air force and the navy, with the loss of maintenance personnel and pilots. The Gripen fighter aircraft that have been arriving cannot be flown. [130] Francois Hugo of the Center for Maritime Technology commented that the navy is sending a corvette to China and has to draw crew from the other corvettes and that three submarines bought from Germany cannot put to sea.[131] Thus, the South African Navy and South African Air Force both need AFRICOM assistance.[132]

Henri Boschoff of the Institute of Security Studies, [133] who is involved in security sector reform in the Democratic Republic of the Congo (DRC) and Burundi, predicted that the ideological objections of the South African government would fade away. The former Minister of Defense Lekota had ―disappeared" (and has now been replaced) and the SANDF is falling apart. The former head of the parliamentary defense committee, Thandi Modise, could be the new Minister and would change the way of doing business and could be favorable towards AFRICOM. The SANDF needs all the help it can get, including from AFRICOM. The South

African Air Force cannot operate without external assistance, as more than 800 technicians have left for Australia in 2008, and there are only 21 pilots qualified to fly the Gripen fighter aircraft.

In regard to security sector reform in the DRC, there is no white paper on defense and no national security strategy, and US and AFRICOM help is needed. As far as the African Standby Force (ASF), there are 18,000 African troops in UN missions, which is enough for two ASF brigades. The United States, EU and UN are more excited about the ASF than the African states and organizations are. External assistance is needed from the United States and AFRICOM, especially for the ASF Rapid Reaction Forces from the five regional economic communities. They need equipment, transport and logistics. One idea is to establish five sub-regional ASF logistics bases.

Greg Mills commented that South Africa does not know what "league it is playing in" – sub-Saharan Africa or SADC. These are two different "ballgames" with different mindsets, requirements, and expectations. South Africa cannot expect peacekeeping operations to work well if the proper mandate is not provided. South African peacekeepers have been placed in unviable situations. Mills said that the reason was for "African solidarity". South Africa was unwilling to push too hard, proving that it "does not do things differently" from other African countries. The Rwandan peacekeepers in Darfur, who were head and shoulders above other forces, asked whey were the South Africans in soft-skinned vehicles. The Rwandans thought that the South Africans were a joke and that there was a lack of concern about the outside world.

South Africa has the hardware but not the will or capacity to do peacekeeping in Africa. There has been an absence of political will when putting troops in the field to give them the proper equipment and rules of engagement. A telling moment was the SANDF strategic positioning conference, when Defense Minister Lekota and the Chief of the SANDF did not even show up to give anticipated addresses. SADC needs AFRICOM in order to help develop the African Standby Force and particularly the SADC brigade of the African Standby Force.

In reacting to reports about South African views on AFRICOM, Lt Col Thornton Schultz, the Air Attaché to South Africa, several South African neighbors do not share South Africa's views regarding AFRICOM and other policy issues, especially Botswana, Lesotho and Swaziland. They realize that AFRICOM can only bring benefits for more funding, training and advocates for development within US government agencies. In public fora, South African officials resort to political position, but individually officials accept the notion. For example, South African officials would not attend a talk by Deputy Assistant Secretary of Defense Theresa Whelan explaining AFRICOM. However, today, the Department of Defense/SANDF Director for Foreign Relations Mafeking wants to talk with US officials about AFRICOM. It must be remembered that South African officials are accustomed to dealing directly with Washington, DC, so AFRICOM represents a step down. Furthermore, South African officials do not understand US combatant commands and how they work and that they cannot commit forces to combat; the Secretary of Defense must authorize the use of force. The intermediate ranks of the SANDF do not like AFRICOM despite hard work to convince officials at the top. The bureaucratic process is ponderous, and the DoD/SANDF Department of Foreign Relations lacks staff, and there is a current of anti-Americanism there. There is a need for the training of career diplomats within South Africa and SADC. Lt Col Schultz ended by commenting on deficiencies within the South African Navy and Air Force, which the United States and AFRICOM may be able to help rectify if asked.

ATTITUDES IN BOTSWANA TOWARDS AFRICOM AND THE UNITED STATES
Government Attitudes

In contrast to South Africa, Botswana government officials studied AFRICOM in early 2007 and eventually came to support the new command. Foreign Minister Phandu Skelemani said that Botswana supported AFRICOM soon after it was explained by American officials.[134] He stated that Botswana had the right to do support AFRICOM and that lectures from South Africa were not effective. In 2007, AFRICOM had been briefed to him as Defense Minister by Ambassador Kate Canavan and US generals. AFRICOM probably was not introduced in the best way. This created the impression that AFRICOM had been created, because the United States wanted to have greater influence. South African Minster of Defense Lekota made the statement that other SADC states should be consulted before one state interacts with AFRICOM. The Botswana position was that the United States needed to clarify exactly what AFRICOM was. AFRICOM was for the benefit of individual states or collectively with SADC states. Botswana told the United States to proceed with the development of AFRICOM.

According to Foreign Minister Skelemani, General Ward is still in the process of clarifying misconceptions about AFRICOM, such as the Botswana air force base being an American base. Foreign Minister Skelemani made clear that any country could use the Thebepatswa Air Base as long as it was in Botswana's interests. This is a case of sour grapes by other counties who disagreed with the idea of AFRICOM. Some SADC states think the presence of AFRICOM would be a destabilizing influence, which may have been pertinent to Zimbabwe but did not understand Lekota's logic and statement. Skelemani said the he did not know why other states saw a danger in AFRICOM. Botswana and other SADC states could only benefit from exercises and collaboration.

In regard to cooperation in reconstructing Zimbabwe, Foreign Minister Skelemani commented that that old defense forces, dominated by ZANU (PF), must be reformed and reeducation, with old ZANLA combatants retiring. Outside assistance is necessary to do this. If Zimbabwe had accepted, SADC would have assisted. Unfortunately, there may not be enough officers within SADC to assist with reorientation of Zimbabwean officers. Angola, Mozambique and Namibia experience similar problems. Zimbabwe clearly needs the help form well-established democracies, including the United States, where the military takes orders from the civilian sector, not vice-versa.

Ross John Sanoto, Director of the Justice, Defense and Security in the Office of the President indicated that the government weighed AFRICOM for months before eventually welcoming it.[135] He commented that a number of African leaders perceived that AFRICOM was coming to Africa to take charge of the continent. However, AFRICOM has long existed in Stuttgart as EUCOM. Nevertheless, some African leaders campaigned against having AFRICOM situated in any African state, dragging the command's name in the mud in order to paint it negatively in the eyes of the public. For Botswana, leaders needed information regarding the scope and intentions. Botswana was viewed as accepting AFRICOM's request to establish its headquarters in the country. However, that was not Botswana's stance. In Zimbabwe and Namibia, the Botswana Defense Force air base at Thebepatswa is known as ―America's biggest base in Africa". These perceptions are difficult to dispel. However, the United States never pronounced its intention to establish a base in Botswana and now has decided not to place AFRICOM on the continent. As a sovereign state, once Botswana has analyzed a proposal and if it serves the people and national interests. Botswana will make whatever decision suits its interests, regardless of its neighbor's perceptions. In terms of engaging with Southern Africa, SADC is not united at the regional level. Sanoto commented that it is best for AFRICOM to engage with individual states. In addition, AFRICOM should assist in developing regional brigades. He concluded that Botswana's approach is for the country to project itself internationally in the same way as Botswana wants to be treated.

Colonel Lawrence Rapula of the Botswana Defense Force and Senior Operations Officer at SADC said that the AFRICOM concept was good, but the United States made the mistake of trying to put the headquarters on the continent.[136] It should have been placed where others will not suffer. The countries that oppose AFRICOM are those that are run by former liberation movements (South Africa, Zimbabwe, Angola, Mozambique and Namibia). The problem with those countries is that they blame others, like the United States and Britain, for their failings. There is a Setswana saying – ―don't hide yourself behind your finger." Don't blame others for your own failures. The former liberation militants feel that they are owed. In contrast, Botswana is a country that was not freed by a liberation movement and the leadership took responsibility for the development of the country and did not blame Britain or the United States for its problems. Instead, Botswana has worked with Britain, the United States and a variety of actors to bring development to the country and to deal with HIV/AIDS and other problems. Therefore, Botswana sees no problem in working with the United States and AFRICOM. The problem is that SADC has been the "big boy's playground" (dominated by Zimbabwe and South Africa), but Botswana is a mature and wise country. For example, other countries are coming to Botswana for training. Namibia came for local government training, and South Africa came for military and security training. Col. Rapula closed by saying that AFRICOM should continue working with African countries. The United States may be able to influence others. However, Botswana will only take what is food for the country. Ultimately, the United States has to conduct effective diplomacy within SADC to gain acceptance for AFRICOM. Engaging with the SADC brigade of the African Standby Force will time as the Zimbabwe issue must first be settled. [137] Most interviewees said that the United States and AFRICOM should work through "reliable" states, such as Botswana, while maintaining good diplomatic relations with SADC and mounting exercises involving SADC. [138]

SADC headquarters are located in Botswana, and the field research included an interview with think tank experts and academics close to SADC decision-makers and administrators. According to Mpho Molomo, a security professor at the University of Botswana, the United States and AFRICOM should work through SADC. [139] Molomo also said that Botswana's government is secretive when it comes to AFRICOM; it is difficult to know what the government is thinking. In regard to public opinion, objections to AFRICOM were aired in the media. In June 2008, when the Botswana chapter of the Africa Center for Strategic Studies hosted a talk on AFRICOM, societal reaction was unfavorable. When Botswana built the Thebepatswa Air Base, the perceptions were that the United States financed it, which the United States denied (France was actually financing it). However, it came to be widely believed that the United States built it to promote regime change in Southern Africa including the ANC regime in South Africa. This created the perception that Botswana was the puppet of the US government. For example, the Voice of America broadcasts from Selebi-Pikwe, which displeases the Zimbabwean government. If Botswana had hosted AFRICOM, this perception would have been reinforced that Botswana was the US "running dog". In 2003, when Botswana signed Article 98, agreeing not to arrest US military personnel and hand them over to the International Criminal Court, it was viewed unfavorably by other states in the region. The government admitted that it was not easy to sign but felt that it had no choice.

The US Charge d'Affaires in Botswana, Rebecca Gonzalez said that Botswana is very keen about AFRICOM. However, some people in the region are "paranoid", talking about a "secret US Air Force base" in Botswana and US troops intervening in the region.[140] An upcoming C-130J visit to the South African show has encountered overflight problems in the region due to these misconceptions. She said that Botswana has taken a "principled approach" to AFRICOM and to Zimbabwe. President Ian Khama has emerged as a regional leader, in spite of the "liberation movement club", and Zambia and Tanzania are siding with Botswana. Thus it seems that Botswana and pro-US SADC states are standing up against South Africa and other states that are headed by former liberation movements.

SADC Attitudes about AFRICOM

J.M. Kaunda,[141] the research director of the FORPRISA[142] think tank that advises SADC, was of two minds about the United States and AFRICOM. On the one hand, he said that SADC did not need US or AFRICOM training and assistance and advised that the United States needs to establish a partnership with SADC, like the European Union has, and avoid being dictatorial. On the other hand, he commented that SADC was poor and dependent on donors and that the bureaucracy was under-resourced and weak. Nevertheless, he advised that the United States and AFRICOM work through SADC rather than individual states. If the United States would offer finding, SADC would be willing to engage with AFRICOM. He admitted that the United States and European Union could do a lot to help Zimbabwe recover from its crisis, something that would provide the basis for improved US-SADC relations.

SOUTH AFRICAN ATTITUDES COMPARED WITH THOSE IN EAST AFRICA

East African policy towards the United States is critical of the US war on terror, and the countries of the region are more supportive of US policy in general. Gilbert Khadiagala, a Kenyan international relations expert at the University of the Witwatersrand,[143] said that South Africa has a different perspective, because it is the "big boy" and influences the rest of SADC. South Africa is not interested in AFRICOM, and attitude that fits into its "love-hate" relationship with the United States. He sees South African non-alignment policy as akin to Cuba's and that Mbeki would not bend to the "US line". He thinks that the transition to new administrations in Pretoria and Washington will create the opportunity for a renewed relationship. A key will be a US ambassador to South Africa who is a skillful diplomat. The United States needs to work state-by-state to win approval for AFRICOM and then engage with SADC, ECOWAS, the EAC and other regional organizations. South Africa is happy to participate in Africa Center for Strategic Studies events. There have been no joint exercises between the United States and SADC for the past ten years due to Zimbabwe and Iraq. ACSS needs to be expanded to do more grassroots work (not just elites)

Kenya would have been inclined to accept AFRICOM and even may have hosted AFRICOM headquarters or a regional office. President Mwai Kibaki was in favor but Raila Odinga (now prime minister) and the opposition were not. The parliamentary defense and foreign relations committee opposed it. Parliament had been debating anti-terrorism legislation, and the announcement of AFRICOM and the aftermath of the US invasion of Iraq muddied the deliberations. The inability to explain and ―sell" AFRICOM made opposition easier. Anti-terrorism legislation is stalled, due to linkage with AFRICOM. US Somali policy was also a factor.

Khadiagala indicated that the mixed Kenyan views on AFRICOM reflect the fact that Kenyan foreign policy does not amount to much, despite a well-educated political elite and diplomatic corps. Kenya needs to develop naval power to deal with piracy and fisheries. There is a need for strategic thinking. However, much of the military training, especially for officers is being done in India where the professional military education is more focused on doctrine and less on strategic thinking. Another issue is the Nile and relations with Egypt. There is no strategic view on water. A Kenyan school of diplomacy has been asked to develop a vision for Kenyan foreign policy. In regard to Southern Sudan and Somalia, policy is badly lacking. There is no national interest in Kenyan foreign policy, just maintenance of status quo. There is no real anti-terrorism policy in Kenya. The bombing of the US embassy in August 1998 made Kenya more cautious rather than pursing those groups responsible for the bombing.

The US 3-D policy in the Horn of Africa is neutralized as long as air and strikes continue to be launched against suspected terrorist bases. It has to be explained better, why the US military has more money to build wells than USAID and the State Department. There is still a lot of resentment against the United States in Garissa – the capital of the Somali region in Kenya. One cannot underestimate the degree of negative attitudes. Al Qaeda and other organizations build on these negative attitudes. A ―hearts and minds" campaign does not really address the problem as people remain very skeptical and are not changing their negative attitudes towards the United States. Also, the reason why the US military is building wells, schools and clinics needs to be better explained.

In regard to other Eastern African countries, the reaction to AFRICOM was mixed, with Tanzania saying no and Uganda and Rwanda reacting positively, though not offering to host. Ethiopia would have been amenable but was worried about a negative reaction by the African

Union (especially given Libya's offer to relocate the AU). He said that the United States needs to put more funding into ACSS.

WEST AFRICA AND CENTRAL AFRICA

Interviewees indicated that West Africa and ECOWAS are less ideological in orientation towards the United States and AFRICOM compared to Southern Africa and SADC. Adekeye Adebajo and Harry Garuba from Nigeria and John Akokpari from Ghana said that West African policy towards the United States is more pragmatic than that of SADC and that the countries in the ECOWAS region are more realistic in their policies than South Africa.[144] Nigeria, as the regional hegemon, helped keep AFRICOM for establishing its headquarters in Liberia. However, once the United States decided not to establish a headquarters on the continent, Nigeria reversed its position and led ECOWAS in accepting AFRICOM.

In Central Africa, France opposes AFRICOM notes Paul-Simon Handy from Cameroon and ISS-Pretoria.[145] In Central Africa, French presence remains quite pronounced, so AFRICOM must seek to coexist with France. Chad would be open to AFRICOM as it would help an illegitimate presence maintain power. No official position and France is lobbying against AFRICOM. The United States started with a bad PR job but has changed considerably so that AFRICOM is perceived more positively.

CONCLUSION

This report has demonstrated that US change agents in seeking transformation focused inwardly within the bureaucracy. They did not bother to consult with African leaders and made assumptions about African reactions to AFRICOM which demonstrated a lack of empathy. The authoritarian leadership style of Rumsfeld brought about an —offer that could not be refused," including the unfortunate directive that AFRICOM headquarters should be placed on the African continent. The directive was rejected by most African leaders and media. A subsequent —strategic communications" campaign to repackage AFRICOM and sell it to African leaders failed because of already established suspicions. Only the reversal of the directive to place the command on the continent brought grudging acceptance, along with US offers of training exercises and other forms of security assistance. Change agents within a bureaucracy must be careful to consult with foreign actors in attempting to bring about transformation. This is easier said than done, especially when the leader of the bureaucracy is authoritarian. Decision-making is not always focused on foreign policy results rather it looks for bureaucratic victories. Thus, if the expected utility of success or failure in implementation is not high, the governmental (bureaucratic) politics model becomes more applicable. A related conclusion has to do with the —American way of diplomacy". The military leads the way with well-resourced and powerful and regionally focused combatant commands. Congress is willing to fund the military and not the State Department and the US Agency for International Development.

While African reaction to AFRICOM was largely negative, there was variation in types of responses. Some leaders in sub-regions and states feared terrorist attacks against an AFRICOM base that would undermine their regimes. Others feared the possibility of regime change. Sub-regional powers, especially South Africa and Nigeria, objected to US military presence in their areas of hegemonic control. Ideology was important, with non-aligned states rejecting AFRICOM and more liberal and pro-Western states accepting it. A second conclusion is that African states are weak. Those states that do not align themselves with the United States feel threatened by it. For some, the ideology of non-alignment is a way to compensate for vulnerability. In regard to the media and public opinion, they have been important in the AFRICOM case, though they remain of secondary importance to the positions of leaders. Also, the feedback to AFRICOM by leading states, such as Nigeria and South Africa, compared to that of sub-regional organizations indicates that the political strength of the latter is incipient and that will remain subordinate to leading states.

The negative lessons of 2007 demonstrate that Africa Command and US diplomats should continue engaging with regional players in order to explain the purpose of the new command and react to feedback. Thanks to considerable US diplomacy in 2008, African perceptions of US security policy and strategy in Africa and of US Africa Command have shifted from largely negative to mostly positive.

In regard to how Africa Command is interacting and can partner with the African Union, Southern African Development Community and other regional organizations in security and development initiatives, AFRICOM is in a supporting role to the Department of State and US ambassadors. In regard to SADC, the United States and AFRICOM have not been relating to SADC because of sanctions against Zimbabwe. It could interact with SADC and Zimbabwe now that a power sharing agreement has been signed and could be implemented. The role of Africa Command in helping to secure resources in Africa is largely maritime in nature, including the prevention and interdiction of piracy and the protection of off-shore and littoral oil assets and fisheries on behalf of African states.

The United States and AFRICOM need to act carefully in shaping efforts throughout Africa to assist in the war on Al Qaeda and terrorism and helping develop and implement strategy that will best use US resources. Africa Command's influence on foreign perceptions of America in Africa has been negative, but a new administration has the chance to make those perceptions more positive. Africa Command should be supportive of State Department efforts in strategic communications in support of US Africa strategy.[146]

Given the variation in attitudes towards AFRICOM across regions and states, it must be concluded that the opinion-shaping strategy of the US State Department and AFRICOM requires region or nation-specific modifications. Interests and ideology differ widely from Southern Africa to other regions. Thus, the message for South Africa and SADC must be different from that for Nigeria and ECOWAS without being contradictory, which is a difficult task. The new administration must work hard to improve relations with South Africa; for instance by reviving the bi-national commission. The United States AFRICOM should work through individual states, such as Botswana, seek to convince South Africa, and establish a working relationship with SADC, the African Union and other organizations.

The viability of AFRICOM in the face of Congressional scrutiny raises the possibility that the new command will not be fully funded. It is probable that African leaders will be disappointed at the likely sub-optimal performance of AFRICOM. As has been demonstrated, US officials visiting African capitals presented messages that AFRICOM would be non-threatening and ―non-kinetic" and would serve African interests by assuming from EUCOM responsibility for peacekeeping and other training and humanitarian activities.[147] In assuring African leaders that AFRICOM would bring no major changes in US policy and posture on the continent, American officials have found it difficult to assert to Congress that the new command would advance US strategic interests. Nevertheless, in order to convince Congress to allocate hundreds of millions of dollars to AFRICOM and its operations, officials stress that the new command would be helping to advance US interests by leading in the war on terror as well as implying that the new command would help protect oil assets and counter China's rise. Officials have emphasized the strategic importance of Africa and stressed that AFRICOM would be as important as other regional combatant commands in protecting and advancing US interests.[148] Thus, US officials have been at cross-purposes in regard to AFRICOM.

After October 1, 2008, AFRICOM will advance US interests through partnerships with African governments, organizations, militaries to enhance security, including training, airlift, and disaster relief. In assisting in the provision of security, AFRICOM will be conducting peacekeeping and counterterrorism training and exercises. One area of focus has been on ―winning hearts and minds", especially in areas under threat from Islamic extremism. At issue is whether AFRICOM will maintain the security and development efforts conducted by CENTCOM's Combined Joint Task Force Horn of Africa (CJTF-HOA) and EUCOM's Trans-Sahara Counter-terrorism Program (TSCTP) in cooperation with African states and organizations.

They may be dismantled because they have not been cost-effective. AFRICOM will have a role in the Africa Contingency Operations Training Assistance (ACOTA) program, especially in regard to exercises, and in assisting in the development of the African Standby Force (ASF). A third area will be the role of Africa Command in working with African states in securing energy resources. For example, AFRICOM could assist Nigeria to improve the security situation in the oil-rich Niger Delta and establishing a more permanent naval presence in the Gulf of Guinea. However, AFRICOM's activities ultimately will be less significant than EUCOM and CENTCOM's and will disappoint African leaders.[149]

ENDNOTES

1 The CENTCOM area of responsibility in Africa included Egypt, Sudan, Eritrea, Ethiopia, Somalia, Seychelles, and Kenya, and the PACOM area Madagascar, Mauritius, and The Comoros. The EUCOM area encompassed the rest of Africa (42 countries).

2 Interviews by the author with members of the AFRICOM Implementation Planning Team, Washington, DC, December 1, 2006 (non-attributable remarks).

3 US STRATCOM Foreign Media Analysis Program, Voices From Africa, Perceptions of the US in African Media, SOS International Ltd., Reston, VA, August 2007.

4 Comments (non-attributable) by US Embassy officials, Addis Ababa, Ethiopia, March 3, 2008.

5 Peter Baker, "No Bases Planned for Africa, Bush Says: President Tries to Ease Concern on Continent Over Expanding Military Presence," Washington Post, February 21, 2008.

6 Charlie Coon, "AFRICOM to rely on local knowledge in lieu of African headquarters", Stars and Stripes, June 29, 2008, 1.

7 "An Overview of President Bush's Africa Strategy", US State Department, July 11, 2003, http://www.state.gov/p/af/rls/22364.htm

8 Graham Allison and Philip Zelikow, The Essence of Decision: Explaining the Cuban Missile Crisis, Second Edition, New York: Addison-Wesley, 1999, 13-75.

9 Allison and Zelikow, The Essence of Decision, 13-75.

10 John Odell, "The U.S. and the Emergence of Flexible Exchange Rates: An analysis of foreign policy change", International Organization, Vol. 33 Issue 1, Winter 1979, 65-90.

11 D. C. Watt, "The Law of the Sea Conference and the Deep Sea Mining Issue: The Need for an Agreement", International Affairs, Vol. 58, No. 1 (Winter, 1981-1982), pp. 78-94. See also, J.B. Morell, The Law of the Sea: An Historical Analysis of the 1982 Treaty and Its Rejection by the United States, McFarland & Company, 1992.

12 Defense Link, www.defenselink.mil/policy/sections/leadership. "The mission of the Office of the Under Secretary of Defense for Policy is to consistently provide responsive, forward-thinking, and insightful policy advice and support to the Secretary of Defense, and the Department of Defense, in alignment with national security objectives." Principal Deputy Under Secretary of Defense for Policy Ryan Henry was especially important in the AFRICOM formation process.

13 Robert D. Kaplan, "What Rumsfeld Got Right", The Atlantic Monthly, July/August 2008, http://www.theatlantic.com/doc/200807/rumsfeld

14 James M. Goldgeier, "NATO Expansion: The Anatomy of a Decision," in The Domestic Sources of American Foreign Policy: Insights and Evidence, 2004, 319–334.

15 Peter Schraeder, United States Foreign Policy towards Africa: Incrementalism, Crisis, and Change, Cambridge: Cambridge University Press, 1994, 11-50.

16 John Kingdon, Agendas, Alternatives and Public Policies, New York: Longman, 2003.

17 Vaughn P. Shannon and Jonathan W. Keller, "Leadership Style and Norm Violation: The Case of the Iraq War", Foreign Policy Analysis, Vol. 3, Issue 1, 2006, 79-104.

18 "Secretary Rumsfeld Speaks on '21st Century Transformation' of U.S. Armed Forces" (transcript of remarks and question and answer period), Remarks as Delivered by Secretary of Defense Donald Rumsfeld, National Defense University, Fort McNair, Washington, D.C., Thursday, January 31, 2002 http://www.defenselink.mil/speeches/speech.aspx?speechid=183

19 Kaplan, "What Rumsfeld Got Right", The Atlantic Monthly, July/August 2008.

20 Allison, Essence, 153-158.

21 Douglas Lemke, "Return to Realism: Power Politics and State Making in Africa", Paper presented at the annual meeting of the International Studies Association 48th Annual Convention, Hilton Chicago, February 28, 2007. See also Lemke, "African Lessons for International Relations Research", World Politics, Volume 56, Number 1, October 2003, pp. 114-138.

22 Rocky Williams, "Don't Hold the African Crisis Response Force to Unrealistic Demands", Institute of Security Studies (Pretoria), Occasional Paper No 20, April 1997, http://www.iss.co.za/index.php?link_id=22&slink_id=682&link_type=12&slink_type=12&tmpl_id=3

23 Interviews in Mali, March 2007, Rwanda, March 2008, and Botswana, August 2008.

24 Amadu Sesay, "Africa, Non-Alignment and the End of the Cold War", in Akinrinade, Sola and Amadu Sesay, eds., Africa in the Post-Cold War International System (London: Pinter, 1998) pp. 147-171.

25 Jakkie Cilliers of the Institute of Security Studies asserted that South Africa was rejecting AFRICOM, because it wanted to maintain its dominance within the Southern African region.

26 Marina Ottaway, Africa's New Leaders: Democracy or State Reconstruction? Washington, DC: Carnegie Endowment for International Peace, 1999, chapter 1.

27 Dana Priest, The Mission: Waging War and Keeping Peace with America's Military, New York: W.W. Norton, 2003, 71-77. James R. Locher, III, Victory on the Potomac: The Goldwater-Nichols Act Unifies the Pentagon, College Station: Texas A & M University Press, 2002, 440-445. The other geographical combatant command is NORTHCOM, founded in the wake of the attacks of September 11, 2001, to provide military assistance to

homeland defense". The basis for NORTHCOM is the North American Air Defense System (NORAD), founded in the 1950s between the United States and Canada. The one difficulty that NORTHCOM has experienced is establishing a relationship with Mexico. See Kaplan, ―What Rumsfeld Got Right".

28 General John Craddock, Commandant, United States Southern Command, remarks at National Defense University, October 31, 2005. ―In the United States, the Command faces the challenge of acquiring sufficient resources to pursue US security interests in the region. Projected funding is below the amount needed for mission-critical operations. One such under-funded critical mission is the ongoing, and multifaceted effort to counter drug trafficking."

29 Sally Donnelly, ―Exclusive: The Pentagon Plans for an African Command", Time Magazine, August 24, 2006.

30 The EUCOM-CENTCOM ―seam" placed Libya, Chad, Central African Republic, Democratic Republic of the Congo, Uganda, and Tanzania on the EUCOM side and Egypt, Sudan, and Kenya on the CENTCOM side. This created operational challenges from 2004 onwards as EUCOM engaged in Darfur, Sudan.

31 John E. Campbell, ―Sub-Saharan Africa and the Unified Command Plan", Joint Forces Quarterly, 2002, Autumn/Winter 2001-2002, 72-75.

32 ―QDR 2001", The Defense Strategy Review Page, http://www.comw.org/qdr/01qdr.html

33 Paul Reynolds, ―US Redeploying for Quicker Action," BBC News, August 16, 2004, http://news.bbc.co.uk/2/hi/americas/3569850.stm. ―Instead of the Cold War idea of basing large numbers of troops to face a known enemy in a predictable place, like Germany, there would be a series of bases strung out across the world like lilies across a pond."

34 Kaplan, ―What Rumsfeld Got Right", The Atlantic Monthly, July/August 2008.

35 ―QDR 2001", The Defense Strategy Review Page, http://www.comw.org/qdr/01qdr.html.

36 Sara Wood, ―Africa Command Will Consolidate US Efforts on Continent," US Federal News Service, February 6, 2007.

37 Briefing, DOD, subject: Changes to the Unified Command Plan to Create an Africa Command, February 7, 2007.

38 Briefing, Foreign Press Center, subject: US to Establish New U.S. Africa Command (AFRICOM), February 9, 2007.

39 Al Pressin, ―VOA News: African Officials Express Concerns About US Africa Command Plan," US Federal News Service, April 23, 2007.

40 Sara Wood, ―Africa Command Gears toward Stability," US Federal News Service, February 7, 2007.

41 Mail & Guardian, South Africa, February 9, 2007.

42 Business Day, South Africa, February 9, 2007.

43 Business Day, SA, February 14, 2007.

44 Darrin Taylor, ―New US Military Command for Africa Stirs Intense Emotion," Voice of America News, October 22, 2007, available at http://www.voanews.com/english/archive/2007-10/New-US-Military-Command-For-Africa-Stirs-Intense-Emotion.cfm?CFID=199535923&CFTOKEN=94823263. Also, interviews in Kenya with military personnel, March 2008.

45 Eze, ―AFRICOM"; A.B. Samori-Toure, ―Africom and the March of the Folly," Leadership (Abuja), January 16, 2008, available at http://allafrica.com/stories/printable/200801160260.html; and interviews with senior Kenyan military officers, Nairobi, March 2008.

46 Interview with Kenyan military officials in Ethiopia, March 2008.

47 Editorial, Mmegi/The Reporter (Gaborone), February 21, 2008, available at http://allafrica.com/stories/ 200802211057.html.

48 Interviews with South African officials in South Africa, August 2008 and in Ethiopia, March 2008.

49 Andrew Kohut, Richard Wike, and Juliana Menasce Horowitz, Global Unease with Major World Powers: 47-Nation Pew Global Attitudes Survey, Pew Research Center, June 27, 2007.

50 Daily Trust, Nigeria, February 11, 2007.

51 Editorial in Daily Trust, Nigeria, February 11, 2007.

52 Ikechukwu Eze, ―AFRICOM: Furore over America's African trail," Business Day, December 24, 2007, available at http://www.businessdayonline.com/analysis/features/1718.html?

53 Eze, ―AFRICOM" and Rosa Brooks, ―Bush's Africa Burden: A sensible U.S. effort to promote stability on the continent may be undermined by using the military to spearhead it," Los Angeles Times, February 21, 2008.

54 Todd Pitman, ―America unifies its troops in Africa: Trojan horse? New U.S. military push into oil-rich continent serves many purposes--and engenders skepticism," Associated Press, November 11, 2007, available at http://www.ajc.com/metro/content/printedition/2007/11/11/afmilitary1111.html; Stratfor, ―Nigeria: Moving for control in the Gulf of Guinea," http://www.ajc.com/metro/content/printedition/ 2007/11/11/afmilitary1111.html; Chinyere Okoye, ―Africom Ship Heads for Gulf of Guinea, January 18, 2008, http://allafrica.com/; and Nnorom Oguchuchukwu, ―US Africom shipped headed for W/Africa," Business Day, January 17, 2008, available at http://www.businessdayonline.com/national/2301.html.

55 AllAfrica.com, June 25, 2007. Mali also indicated an interest in hosting AFRICOM.

56 ―Lekota: Africom should stay off the continent" Mail and Guardian (South Africa), August 29, 2007, http://www.mg.co.za/article/2007-08-29-lekota-africom-should-stay-off-the-continent

57 Daniel Gordon, ―The controversy over Africom," BBC World Service's Analysis Programme, October 3, 2007, available at http://news.bbc.co.uk/2/hi/africa/7026197.stm.

58 Fabricius, ―SADC Shuns Spectre of US Africom Plans."

59 Jakkie Cilliers.

60 Peter Fabricius, ―SADC Shuns Spectre of US Africom Plans," Sunday Independent, 15 July 2007, available at http://www.iol.co.za/general/news/newsprint.php/art_id=un20070715084547855C635785.

61 Discussions with South African officials and academics, August 2008.

62 Mmegi/The Reporter, Botswana, February 27, 2007.

63 Mmegi/The Reporter, Botswana, February 28, 2007.

64 Kitseile Nyathi, ―Southern Africa: AFRICOM Plans in Botswana Causes Tension," Daily Nation (Kenya), September 13, 2007, http://allafrica.com/. There is a widespread rumor that the Thebe-patswa Air Base in Botswana was built as a US military base from which US forces could stage regime change in Zimbabwe and elsewhere in SADC.

G. Dunkel, ―U.S. military interventions arouse African suspicions," Workers World, September 9, 2007, available at http://www.workers.org/print.php.

65 Peter Fabricius, ―SADC Shuns Spectre of US Africom Plans," Sunday Independent, July 15, 2007, available at http://www.iol.co.za/general/news/newsprint.php/art_id=un20070715084547855C635785. G. Dunkel, ―U.S. military interventions arouse African suspicions"; and Kitseile Nyathi, ―Southern Africa: AFRICOM Plans in Botswana Causes Tension.

66 Daily Nation, Kenya, February 8, 2007.

67 East African Standard, Kenya, May 27, 2007.

68 Discussions with Rwandan President Paul Kagame and senior Rwandan Defense Force officers, March 2008.

69 Simon Tisdall, ―African States Oppose Us Presence," Guardian Unlimited, June 25, 2007; The News (Monrovia), ―Liberia: Johnson Sirleaf 'Offers' Territory for Africom Headquarters," July 6, 2007, http://allafrica.com/; Ellen Johnson Sirleaf, ―Africa: Africom Can Help Governments Willing to Help Themselves," June 25, 2007, http://allafrica.com/.

70 Al Tajdid, Morocco, June 12, 2007.

71 El Watan, Algeria, March 3, 2007

72 Al Ahram, Egypt, June 14, 2007.

73 Todd Pitman, ―America unifies its troops in Africa: Trojan horse? New U.S. military push into oil-rich continent serves many purposes."

74 Craig Whitlock, ―North Africa Reluctant to Host US Command: Algeria and Libya Reject Pentagon's Africom Proposal Morocco Signals Its Lack of Enthusiasm," Washington Post, June 24, 2007; Todd Pitman, ―America unifies its troops in Africa: Trojan horse? New U.S. military push into oil-rich continent serves many purposes--and engenders skepticism," Associated Press, November 11, 2007, available at http://www.ajc.com/metro/content/printedition/2007/11/11/afmilitary1111.html; 2007/11/11/afmilitary1111.html.

75 Al Pressin, ―African officials express concerns about U.S. Africa Command Plan," US Fed News Service, April 23, 2007.

76 David Ignatius, ―Growing US Military Role in Africa," Denver Post, January 3, 2008.

77 Charles Kozak, Director, Office of the Secretary of Defense for Africa, May 15, 2007 briefing at Air War College, Alabama.

78 Al Pressin, ―The United States Creates Military Command for Africa," DISAM Journal of International Security Assistance Management 29 (July 2007): 84.

79 Jendayi Frazer, Assistant Secretary for African Affairs, Senate Committee of Foreign Relations, August 1, 2007 [http://www.state.gov/p/af/rls/rm/89905.htm].

80 Steven Donald Smith, ―Africa Command Poised to Help Continent's Security, Stability." American Forces Press Service, September 21, 2007.

81 Jim Fisher-Thompson, ―State Department: US Africa Command Will Enhance Local Skills, Problem Solving."

82 Smith, ―Africa Command Poised to Help Continent's Security, Stability."

83 Gregory E. Glaros, ―The New Africa Command: A Hedge against Neo-Colonialism or a True Agent of Change?" Signal, 62 (September 2007): 120.

84 Jim Fisher-Thompson, ―State Department: U.S. Africa Command Will Enhance Local Skills, Problem Solving," US Federal News Service, September 28, 2007.

85 Rosa Brooks, ―Bush's Africa Burden."

86 Peter Baker, ―No Bases Planned for Africa, Bush Says: President Tries to Ease Concern on Continent Over Expanding Military Presence," Washington Post, February 21, 2008.

87 Interviews in Ethiopia, Rwanda, and Kenya, March 2008. Field research in East Africa found the widespread desire to develop African solutions for African problems and shared US-African goals of peace and security, economic, health care and education development and capacity building. Discontent over the US failure to adequately engage African heads of state underscored why the AFRICOM concept was misunderstood and rejected.

88 I would like to thank Janet Beilstein of the International Officers School at Air University for her assistance in this research. This research on AFRICOM follows on field research over the past three years on the African Standby Force and the African Union Peace and Security Council and Peace Operations in Africa.

89 United States Diplomatic Mission to Nigeria, ―Closing Ceremony Marks End of Successful Africa Endeavor 2008", July 23, 2008, http://nigeria.usembassy.gov/prog_07232008.html. The exercise in Nigeria included AFRICOM and militaries from 25 African states, which was proof that a majority accepted AFRICOM and exercises with the US military.

90 International Law Enforcement Agency, Gaborone. http://www.ileagaborone.co.bw/ILEA%20Courses.html. A course was held from July 28 to September 5, 2008.

91 Lt Col Thornton Schultz, US Air Attaché to South Africa, interviewed August 11, 2008.

92 Presentation, ―The Future of US Africa Relations", by Stephen Burgess at the Center for International Policy Studies symposium, Pretoria, South Africa, August 6, 2008 and comments by South African government officials in attendance. Non-attribution rules applied.

93 Presentation by Burgess and comments by South African officials.

94 Presentation by Burgess and comments by South African officials.

95 Presentation by Burgess and comments by South African officials.

96 Presentation by Burgess and comments by South African officials.

97 The expression ―ideology of non-alignment" can be seen as a euphemism for anti-Americanism generated by African National Congress officials, many of whom had returned in the 1990s from exile in the Soviet Union, Cuba, East Germany, Angola and other communist countries. Also, it must be remembered that the South African Communist Party remains allied with the ruling African National Congress.

98 Wafula Okumu, Institute of Security Studies, Pretoria is a leading critic of AFRICOM and testified before the US House of Representatives in August 2007.

99 Garth le Pere, Siphamandla Zondi, Lyal White and Francis N. Ikome, Institute for Global Dialogue (IGD), interviewed August 8, 2008, Midrand Johannesburg, South Africa. In addition, Michelle Reitus is the AFRICOM expert at IGD. Adekeye Adebajo, Centre for Conflict Resolution, interviewed August 14, 2008, Cape Town, South Africa. Richard Cornwell, Institute of Security Studies, interviewed August 5, 2008, Pretoria, South Africa. Harry Stephan, Department of Politics, University of Cape Town, interviewed August 14, 2008. Also critical of AFRICOM is Wafula Okumu of ISS-Pretoria, who testified before Congress in August 2007 against the new command.

100 Zondi, IGD, August 8, 2008,

101 Zondi, IGD, August 8, 2008. The ―3d" concept has been introduced as a result of US counterinsurgency operations in Afghanistan, Iraq and the Horn of Africa.

102 Sean McFate, ―Briefing: US Africa Command: Next Step or Next Stumble?" African Affairs, Volume 107, Number 426, January 2008, pp. 111-120.

103 Harry Stephan, Department of Politics, University of Cape Town, interviewed August 14, 2008

104 Zondi, IGD, August 8, 2008.

105 Ikome, IGD, August 8, 2008.

106 Adebajo, CCR, August 14, 2008.

107 In reality, there are only 500 troops stationed at CJTF-HOA headquarters at Camp Lemonier.

108 Greg Mills, Brenthurst Foundation, interviewed August 8, 2008, Johannesburg, South Africa.

109 Greg Mills, August 8, 2008.

110 Francois Vrey and Abel Esterhuyse, faculty, South African Military Academy and University of Stellenbosch interviewed August 15, 2008 in Saldanha, South Africa.

111 Gavin Cawthra, Director of the Centre for Defence and Security Management, University Of Witwatersrand, interviewed August 6, 2008, Johannesburg.

112 Gavin Cawthra, August 6, 2008.

113 Naison Ngoma, ISS, interviewed August 5, 2008.

114 Vrey and Esterhuyse, August 15, 2008. For example, private security is the second largest employer after the oil industry in Nigeria. Also, there is a growing private security in South Africa with growing crime.

115 Mark Malan has written about the problems of no quality control over private contractors.

116 Richard Cornwell, ISS.

117 Richard Cornwell in subsequent comments said that President Bashir of Sudan is privately worried about the ICC. Sudan is subject to the Rome Statute through a UNSC resolution 1593 (2003).

118 Zondi, IGD, August 8, 2008.

119 Renfrew Christie, Dean, School of Social Sciences, University of the Western Cape, interviewed August 14, 2008, Cape Town, South Africa.

120 Chris Landsberg, University of Johannesburg, interviewed September 2005.

121 Greg Mills and Terence McNamee, ―The Fall of Mbeki", International Herald Tribune, September 25, 2008, http://www.iht.com/articles/2008/09/25/opinion/edmills.php

122 Richard Cornwell, August 5, 2008.

123 Brooks Spector, consultant and former US Information Service official, interviewed August 11, 2008, Johannesburg, South Africa.

124 Francis Kornegay, Centre for Policy Studies, interviewed August 8, 2008, Johannesburg, South Africa.

125 Kgalema Motlanthe has become interim president of South Africa, with the expectation that Jacob Zuma will become president in May 2009. Charles Nqakula, an ANC veteran, has become Minister of Defense and F Bhengu, the former chairperson of the Portfolio Committee on Defence, Deputy Minister of Defense. Dr NC Dlamini-Zuma will remain as Minister of Foreign Affairs with Aziz GH Pahad the deputy.

126 Deon Geldenhuys, Department of Politics, University of Johannesburg, interviewed August 11, 2008. Mbeki was like Jan Smuts before 1948 – too focused on foreign affairs.

127 Mills, ―The Fall of Mbeki".

128 Roger Southall, Department of Sociology, University of the Witwatersrand, interviewed August 8, 2008, Johannesburg, South Africa.

129 African Crisis Response Initiative and Africa Contingency Training Assistance program.

130 Helmoed Romer Heitman, Jane's Defence Weekly, interviewed August 15, 2008, Cape Town, South Africa. Brig Gen Wiseman Mbambo, South African Air Force, interviewed August 12, 2008; Pretoria, South Africa commented that the air force was undergoing ―growing pains".

131 Francois Hugo, Director, Centre for Maritime Technology, interviewed August 13, 2008, Cape Town, South Africa. Stephen Stead, retired admiral, Brenthurst Foundation, interviewed August 8, 2008, Johannesburg.

132 Heitman and Hugo.

133 Henri Boschoff, Institute of Security Studies, Pretoria, interviewed August 8, 2008. He pointed out that Anglophone doctrine dominates UN and AU peacekeeping missions and suggested that South African doctrine might be better. As far as strategic planning for the ASF, the Strategic Indicative Plan of the SADC Organ on Politics, Defense and Security might be a guide.

134 Foreign Minister Phandu Skelemani interviewed August 21, 2008, Gaborone, Botswana.

135 Ross John Sanoto, Director of the Justice, Defense and Security in the Office of the President, interviewed August 20, 2008, Gaborone, Botswana.

136 Colonel Lawrence Rapula, Botswana Defence Force and SADC interviewed August 21, 2008, Gaborone, Botswana.

137 Similar views were expressed by Col Placid Sekogko, Botswana Defense Force, interviewed August 22, 2008, Gaborone, Botswana.

138 Colonel Placid Sekogko, Botswana Defense Force Air Arm, interviewed August 22, 2008, Gaborone, Botswana.

139 Mpho Molomo, Department of Politics, University of Botswana, interviewed August 20, 2008, Gaborone, Botswana.

140 US Charge d'Affaires in Botswana, Rebecca Gonzalez, interviewed August 22, 2008.

141 J. Mayuyuka Kaunda, Senior Researcher, BIDPA/FORPRISA, interviewed August 22, 2008.

142 Formative Process Research on Integration in Southern Africa – Research for Regional Integration and Development – hosted by the Botswana Institute for Development Policy Analysis.

143 Gilbert Khadiagala, August 7, 2008, formerly of the Johns Hopkins School of Advanced International Studies.

144 Adebajo, August 14, 2008. John Akokpari, Department of Politics, University of Cape Town, South Africa, interviewed August 14, 2008. Harry Garuba, associate professor, Centre for African Studies, University of Cape Town, South Africa, interviewed August 18, 2008.

145 Paul-Simon Handy, Institute of Security Studies, interviewed August 8, 2008, Pretoria, South Africa

146 Brooks Spector, August 12, 2008

147 ―AFRICOM Posture Statement: Ward Updates Congress on US Africa Command―‚ Africa Command Public Affairs Office, Washington, D.C. March 13, 2008.

148 ―Transcript: Congress Reconvenes for Second Part of U.S. Africa Command Hearing", House of Representatives Oversight and Government Reform Committee, Washington, D.C., July 28, 2008http://www.africom.mil/getArticle.asp?art=1948

www.ingramcontent.com/pod-product-compliance
Lightning Source LLC
Chambersburg PA
CBHW081538280526
45788CB00010B/3276